Order Code RL32870

CRS Report for Congress

Received through the CRS Web

European Union's Arms Embargo on China: Implications and Options for U.S. Policy

I0415808

Updated May 27, 2005

Kristin Archick
Specialist in European Affairs
Foreign Affairs, Defense, and Trade Division

Richard F. Grimmett
Specialist in National Defense
Foreign Affairs, Defense, and Trade Division

Shirley Kan
Specialist in National Security Policy
Foreign Affairs, Defense, and Trade Division

Congressional Research Service ❖ The Library of Congress

European Union's Arms Embargo on China: Implications and Options for U.S. Policy

Summary

The European Union (EU) is considering lifting its arms embargo on China, which was imposed in response to the June 1989 Tiananmen Crackdown. France, Germany, and other EU members claim that the embargo hinders the development of a "strategic partnership" with China. The Bush Administration and Members of Congress strongly oppose an end to the EU's arms embargo and urge stronger arms export controls. The United States contends that engagement with China need not send the wrong signals on China's human rights record and military buildup that threatens a peaceful resolution of Taiwan and other Asian issues.

The EU argues that the arms embargo — which is not legally binding — is weak and largely symbolic. Indeed, some EU members reportedly have allowed defense-related exports to China under the arms embargo. While such sales have raised questions about the effectiveness of the EU's arms embargo on China, they also point to the potential for future sales of military equipment or technology to China, particularly without the political restraint of the embargo. EU governments, led by the United Kingdom, stress that if and when the embargo is overturned, its end would be accompanied by a stronger EU arms export control regime — including an enhanced EU Code of Conduct on Arms Exports — that will improve accountability and better control arms sales to China and elsewhere. U.S. critics, however, remain skeptical that even a tighter EU Code will contain sufficient enforcement and transparency mechanisms to dissuade EU countries from exporting advanced defense technologies that could enhance China's military buildup and ultimately threaten common U.S., European, and Asian interests in peace and stability.

Many observers had expected that the EU would lift the embargo in the spring of 2005, but this timeline is now in doubt. All 25 EU member states must agree before the embargo can be overturned, but some members appear to be less supportive of ending the embargo amid vocal and high-level U.S. opposition, especially since early 2005. Those arguing against lifting the embargo have cited persistent human rights problems in China, including a refusal to reexamine the Tiananmen Crackdown, and China's adoption in March 2005 of its "Anti-Secession Law" warning of a possible use of force against Taiwan. Still, the EU is politically committed to overturning the embargo, and many observers believe that its end is ultimately only a matter of time. In the meantime, U.S. diplomacy could be effective, and the disagreement presents a chance for closer coordination of U.S.-European policies, including those dealing with arms export controls and a rising China.

Overall, there are two sets of questions for Congress in examining U.S. policy toward the fate of the EU's arms embargo on China. What are the implications for U.S. interests in trans-Atlantic relations and China? If U.S. interests are adversely affected, what are some options for Congress to discourage the EU from lifting its arms embargo on China and, if it is lifted, to protect U.S. national security interests in both Asia and Europe? Issues raised by these questions are the subject of this CRS Report. This report will be updated as warranted.

Contents

Background: Policy Dilemmas 1

Congressional Concerns 2

Decisions on Arms Sanctions 4
    U.S. Sanctions on Arms Sales to China 4
    EU's Arms Embargo on China 5
    Current Status: PRC Pressure on the EU to End Embargo 6
    Administration's Position on the Embargo 8

China's Accelerated Military Buildup 11
    Rising Military Budgets 12
    Military-Related Transfers to China 13
    Potential Benefits for China 15

EU's Perspectives 18
    Political Motivations 18
    Commercial Interests 19
    A Symbolic Embargo? 20
    Code of Conduct and Arms Export Control Regime 21

EU's Plans and Other Options 23

Implications for U.S. Interests 26
    Transatlantic Relations 26
    U.S. Policy Toward China 30

Options for U.S. Policy 33
    Continue to Urge the EU to Maintain its Arms Embargo 33
    Encourage the EU to Strengthen its Code of Conduct 33
    Promote a Cooperative U.S.-EU Strategy 33
    Pursue Robust Bilateral Efforts on European Arms Exports 34
    Engage with the European Parliament 34
    Retaliate to Protect U.S. National Security 34
        Impose Restrictions on Sales of Defense Articles and Technology to
            EU Member States 34
        Impose Restrictions on U.S. Military Procurement from EU States . . 35

Legislation 35
    ITAR Waivers 35
    Defense Procurement Sanctions 35
    Resolutions Urging the EU to Keep the Embargo 36

Appendix: Non-Russian Military-Related Transfers to China 37

List of Tables

Table 1. China's Acquisitions under Reported Contracts for
Military-Related Systems from Europe (Excluding Russia),
Israel, and Others Since the 1990s 37
Table 2. China's Reported Negotiations for Military-Related Systems from
Non-Russian Sources Since the 1990s 42

List of Figures

Figure 1. China's Announced Military Budget 13

European Union's Arms Embargo on China: Implications and Options for U.S. Policy

Background: Policy Dilemmas

The European Union (EU) is considering lifting its arms embargo on the People's Republic of China (PRC), imposed after the June 1989 Tiananmen Square crackdown.[1] Many countries imposed sanctions on China, after Deng Xiaoping and other PRC rulers ordered the military, the People's Liberation Army (PLA), to violently suppress peaceful demonstrators in Beijing on June 4, 1989. (Although the killing of demonstrators took place beyond the Tiananmen Square in the capital of Beijing, the crackdown is commonly called the Tiananmen Crackdown in reference to the square that was the focal point of the nation-wide pro-democracy movement.)

The Bush Administration opposes an end to the EU's arms embargo on China, seeing it as a relaxation in the EU's human rights and arms export policies toward China, and out of step with U.S. sanctions on arms sales to China that have remained since 1989. Overall, there are two sets of questions for Congress in examining U.S. policy toward this question. What are the implications for U.S. political and security interests concerning Europe and China? If U.S. interests are adversely affected, what are some options for Congress to discourage the EU from lifting its arms embargo on China and, if it is lifted, to protect U.S. national security interests? The purpose of this CRS Report is to discuss U.S. concerns and implications for U.S. interests, as the EU considers the future of the arms embargo, as well as options for U.S. policy.

Given strenuous U.S. objections, there are concerns that a decision made by the EU to expand engagement with China by lifting the arms embargo would negatively impact the trans-Atlantic alliance (if there is a division in U.S. and European approaches toward China) and defense cooperation (if the United States responds by restricting technology transfers to Europe or defense procurement from Europe). At the same time, the current disagreement presents an opportunity for closer coordination of U.S.-European policies, including controls over military-related exports and strategy towards China. The United States has important interests in maintaining strong alliances with common approaches toward a rising China.

Like Europe, Washington increasingly has engaged Beijing on the economic, political, and military fronts. A fundamental issue, then, has been how engagement

---

[1] The 25 members of the EU are: Austria, Belgium, Cyprus, the Czech Republic, Denmark, Estonia, Finland, France, Germany, Greece, Hungary, Ireland, Italy, Latvia, Lithuania, Luxembourg, Malta, the Netherlands, Poland, Portugal, Slovakia, Slovenia, Spain, Sweden, and the United Kingdom. Also see CRS Report RS21372, *The European Union: Questions and Answers*, by Kristin Archick.

is pursued and whether it contributes to a more responsible China in domestic and international affairs or aggravates developments in China with adverse implications. For decades, U.S.-PRC relations have expanded with trade and cooperation on international issues. There remain Western concerns, however, about restrictions on human rights and democracy in China, and about the impact of China's weapons proliferation practices and military buildup on peace and stability in Asia and other regions around the world.

Because some European companies have transferred defense-related systems to China under the arms embargo that is not legally binding, the United States has called for the EU to maintain the embargo and strengthen export controls. There are fears that any acceleration of China's military modernization with European defense technology would result in instability in the Taiwan Strait, which could involve U.S. military intervention. This concern stems from one dilemma for U.S. policy: adherence to the "one China" policy since the Nixon Administration started secret talks with the PRC in 1971 while maintaining diplomatic relations with the Republic of China (commonly called Taiwan) until 1979 and unofficial relations since then.

Taiwan remains the major U.S.-PRC issue that could bring the countries into conflict. The 1979 Taiwan Relations Act (TRA), P.L. 96-8, governs U.S. policy toward Taiwan, including offering arms to assist its self-defense. The TRA did not commit the President and Congress to determine any decision to intervene in the event of threats to Taiwan, other than to consider any non-peaceful efforts to determine Taiwan's future "of grave concern to the United States." Nonetheless, among the stipulations of U.S. policy, the TRA declared that it is U.S. policy "to maintain the capacity of the United States to resist any resort to force or other forms of coercion that would jeopardize the security, or the social or economic system, of the people on Taiwan."[2] Thus, in addition to issues about arms sales to Taiwan and the extent of any U.S. commitment to help defend Taiwan, one question is whether the U.S. forces have the capability to deter or defeat the PLA, not only in the event of a use of force but also coercion against Taiwan. Maintenance of cross-strait stability has required a careful balance of ties with both the PRC and Taiwan. There have been periodically heightened tensions between the PRC and Taiwan since the Taiwan Strait Crisis of 1995-1996, sensitive assertions of a separate national identity in Taiwan since 1999, and President Bush's articulation of stronger U.S. support for Taiwan's self-defense in 2001, later qualified by criticism of Taiwan's president in 2003 for perceived attempts to change the cross-strait status quo.

Congressional Concerns

Congress exercises oversight of the effectiveness of the Bush Administration's diplomacy toward Europe. Since 2004, U.S. officials have pressured EU member states not to lift the arms embargo. Congress has supported this stance.

---

[2] See CRS Report RL30341, *China/Taiwan: Evolution of the "One China" Policy — Key Statements from Washington, Beijing, and Taipei*; and CRS Report RL30957, *Taiwan: Major U.S. Arms Sales Since 1990*, by Shirley Kan.

Congress also has expressed concerns about policy toward China, including promotion of human rights. Moreover, Congress has expressed increasing concerns about the PLA's modernization, particularly following the military exercises and missile launches targeted against Taiwan in 1995-1996. Because many EU member states have narrowly interpreted the arms embargo as banning only lethal weapons, some EU countries have sold defense-related technology to China. There is concern that without the arms embargo, EU countries might sell additional dual-use technology and/or weapons systems to China. The PLA could then employ European technology and weapons against U.S. forces and friends, in the event of a conflict with China. Moreover, there is concern about the potential for EU companies involved in U.S.-European defense cooperation to transfer U.S. defense technology to China, undermining U.S. export controls and sanctions on arms sales to China.

In May 2004, the House passed its version of the National Defense Authorization Act for FY2005 (H.R. 4200), reported out of the House Armed Services Committee, which included a provision to impose procurement sanctions against any foreign person that transfers certain military items to China. (Also see section on **Legislation** below.)

In early 2005, Senator Richard Lugar warned that "the technology the U.S. shares with European allies could be in jeopardy if allies were sharing that through these commercial sales with the Chinese."[3] Senator Joseph Biden said that lifting the embargo is "a non-starter with Congress."[4] In the House, Representative Henry Hyde wrote that "the choice for Europe could not be clearer: it is between policies that promote the development of democracy in China or those that support China's military buildup and threaten U.S. security interests."[5]

At a hearing of the Senate Foreign Relations Committee on March 16, 2005, Senator Lugar cautioned that if European military-related transfers to China rises markedly, "we should reassess sales to Europe of our most critical military technology." Referring to China's adoption two days earlier of its "Anti-secession Law" threatening the use of force against Taiwan and raising cross-strait tensions, Senator Lugar counseled that "this is no time to be taking steps that might either help China achieve a decisive military advantage over Taiwan or send the wrong political signal." Likewise, Senator Biden urged the Europeans to maintain the embargo as well as strengthen the Code of Conduct on arms sales, particularly given the timing when the Bush Administration "has reached out to try to begin to mend our frayed relationships with our European allies...."[6]

---

[3] Edward Alden and Demetri Sevastopulo, "Lugar Threat on EU Arms Sales to China," *Financial Times*, February 21, 2005.

[4] Thom Shanker and David Sanger, "U.S. Lawmakers Warn Europe On Arms Sales to China," *New York Times*, March 2, 2005.

[5] Henry Hyde, "Don't Sell Arms To China," *Wall Street Journal*, February 23, 2005.

[6] Senate Foreign Relations Committee, "Hearing on Lifting the EU Arms Embargo on China," March 16, 2005.

Convening a joint hearing in April 2005, Representatives Duncan Hunter, Ike Skelton, Henry Hyde, and Tom Lantos, the Chairs and Ranking Members of the House Armed Services and International Relations Committees expressed their opposition to an end to the EU's arms embargo.[7]

Decisions on Arms Sanctions

U.S. Sanctions on Arms Sales to China

Between 1985 and 1987, the United States had agreed to extend to China four programs of Foreign Military Sales (FMS): modernization of artillery ammunition production facilities; modernization of avionics in F-8 fighters (called the "Peace Pearl" program); sale of four Mark-46 anti-submarine torpedoes; and sale of four AN/TPQ-37 artillery-locating radars.[8] However, in response to the Tiananmen Crackdown, the United States suspended military-to-military contacts and arms sales. First imposed by President George H.W. Bush on June 5, 1989, the ban on arms sales was later codified among sanctions passed in Section 902 of the Foreign Relations Authorization Act for FYs 1990 and 1991 (P.L. 101-246), approved in February 1990. Faced with the sanctions, in April 1990, China canceled the "Peace Pearl" program to upgrade the avionics of the F-8 fighters.[9] In December 1992, President Bush decided to close out the four suspended FMS programs, returning PRC equipment, reimbursing unused funds, and delivering sold items without support.[10]

Congress has oversight of these sanctions that continue to prohibit the issuance of licenses under the Arms Export Control Act to export Munitions List items to China, explicitly including helicopters and helicopter parts; crime control and detection equipment; as well as satellites exported for PRC launch. In certain cases, Presidents have exercised the waiver authority "in the national interest" to export sanctioned items to China. Presidents Bush and Clinton issued 13 waivers for 20 satellite projects from 1989 to 1998.[11] In January 2002, President George W. Bush issued two waivers of the Tiananmen sanctions to export a bomb containment and disposal unit for the Shanghai fire department to prevent terrorist bombings and to export equipment to clean up chemical weapons left in China by Japan in World War II.[12] In September 2003, President Bush issued a waiver of the sanctions to allow the

---

[7] Joint Hearing of the House Armed Services and International Relations Committees, "the National Security and Foreign Policy Implications for the United States of Arms Exports to the People's Republic of China by Member States of the European Union," April 14, 2005.

[8] Department of State and Defense Security Assistance Agency, "Congressional Presentation for Security Assistance, Fiscal Year 1992."

[9] *Jane's Defense Weekly*, May 26, 1990.

[10] State Department, "Presidential Decision on Military Sales to China," December 22, 1992.

[11] CRS Report 98-485, *China: Possible Missile Technology Transfers Under U.S. Satellite Export Policy — Actions and Chronology*, by Shirley Kan.

[12] CRS Report RS21995, *U.S.-China Counter-Terrorism Cooperation: Issues for U.S.*

(continued...)

export to China of QRS-11 sensors that serve as components of inertial measurement units (IMU) used in Boeing commercial aircraft, with export approvals that raised concerns with the Chairman and Ranking Member of the House International Relations Committee.[13]

EU's Arms Embargo on China

European countries took action that corresponded to steps taken by the United States earlier in June 1989 to respond to the Tiananmen Crackdown. The EU arms embargo on China is based on one sentence in a political declaration issued on June 27, 1989, by the then-12 member European Community, the EU's precursor. The declaration condemns the "brutal repression" taking place in China, requests that the Chinese authorities cease executions and respect human rights, and contains measures agreed by the member states. These include the suspension of military cooperation and high-level contacts, reduction of cultural, scientific and technical cooperation programs, and the prolongation of visas to Chinese students. The specific wording of the arms restrictions on China calls for "interruption by the member states of the Community of military cooperation and an embargo on trade in arms with China."[14]

While the EU's June 1989 declaration on China is not legally binding, it represents a political commitment that all EU members are supposed to uphold and enforce.[15] Each EU member, however, defines and implements the arms embargo differently; this has allowed some EU countries to continue to export certain types of military equipment to China despite the embargo. According to the EU, the embargo does not cover a large proportion of "sensitive items," which are covered by other EU legal mechanisms.[16] These on-going sales to China have raised questions about the effectiveness of the EU's arms embargo on China and the EU's wider defense export control policies.

---

[12] (...continued)
Policy, by Shirley Kan.

[13] President George W. Bush, "Waiver of Suspensions With Respect to the Issuance of Licenses for QRS-11 Sensors," September 24, 2003; Letter to Secretary of State Colin Powell from Representatives Tom Lantos and Henry Hyde of the House Committee on International Relations, October 10, 2003; Bill Gertz, "Boeing Sale to China Skirts Ban on Technology Transfer," *Washington Times*, February 5, 2004; House International Relations Committee, hearing on the Budget Request for International Affairs, February 11, 2004.

[14] See the Madrid European Council, Presidency Conclusions, June 27, 1989, available at [http://www.eurunion.org/legislat/Sanctions.htm].

[15] For information on the legal basis of the EU's arms embargo on China and the EU's legal regime on arms exports, see the Law Library of Congress Report No. 2005-01586, *European Union Arms Embargo on China*, by Theresa Papademetriou.

[16] European Union, Fact Sheet, "EU Arms and Dual Use Exports Policy and EU Embargo on China," February 2005 [http://europa.eu.int/comm/external_relations/us/bush/china.pdf].

Current Status: PRC Pressure on the EU to End Embargo

Since 2003, China has been increasing pressure on the EU to end the embargo. In October 2003, China issued its "Policy Paper on the EU," urging the EU to lift its arms embargo in order to "remove barriers to greater bilateral cooperation in defense industries and technology."[17] The EU began reexamining the arms embargo in early 2004.[18] France and Germany have been key drivers of this review process.

The EU-China summit on December 8, 2004, came three days before crucial elections in Taiwan, for which its president campaigned (unsuccessfully) to win a majority for his coalition in the legislature that some feared would lead to constitutional changes considered by Beijing to provocatively push for de jure independence. The EU decided to maintain the embargo at that sensitive time, although it asserted its "political intention to continue to work towards lifting the embargo." China welcomed this "positive signal" for development of the "comprehensive strategic partnership" with the EU.[19]

The decision to end the EU arms embargo rests with the member states of the Union and requires unanimity. In other words, all member states of the now-25 member EU must agree before the arms embargo can be lifted. At the December 16-17, 2004 meeting of EU heads of state and government in Brussels, EU leaders "reaffirmed the political will to continue to work toward lifting the arms embargo."[20] The EU did not state a firm date for ending the embargo, but statements by EU officials strongly suggested that the embargo would be lifted in the spring of 2005.

France and Germany have been key proponents of ending the EU arms embargo on China. Other member states have been more hesitant. The United Kingdom (U.K.) and the Netherlands have shared U.S. concerns about the strategic implications of an end to the embargo, while some of the Scandinavian countries and other smaller states with strong human rights advocacy policies have also been less enthusiastic. But by early 2005, sufficient consensus appeared to have been built up among EU members to lift the embargo in May or June 2005. The willingness of the U.K. and others to overturn the embargo appeared based on their view that the embargo itself was largely ineffective and that it would only be lifted if a stronger EU export control regime was put in place at the same time. Some observers also suggest that London was eager to burnish its European credentials and keen to avoid another fight with Paris and Berlin so soon after their rift over the war in Iraq.

However, press reports and discussions with European officials indicate that it later became unlikely that the EU will move ahead with lifting the embargo in the spring of 2005. EU officials attribute the apparent delay largely to the PRC's "Anti-

---

[17] *Xinhua* [New China News Agency], October 13, 2003.

[18] *EU Business*, December 12, 2003; Craig Smith, "France Makes Headway in Push to Permit Arms Sales to China," *New York Times*, January 27, 2004.

[19] "Joint Statement of the Seventh EU-China Summit," December 8, 2004.

[20] See the Brussels European Council, Presidency Conclusions, December 17, 2004 [http://ue.eu.int/ueDocs/cms_Data/docs/pressData/en/ec/83201.pdf].

Secession Law," warning of the use of force against perceived efforts at establishing Taiwan's independence. On March 14, 2005, China adopted its "Anti-Secession Law," declaring in Article 8 that:

> If the separatist forces of "Taiwan independence" use any name or any means to cause the fact of Taiwan's separation from China, or a major incident occurs that would lead to Taiwan's separation from China, or the possibilities of peaceful unification are completely exhausted, the country may adopt non-peaceful means and other necessary measures to safeguard national sovereignty and territorial integrity.[21]

The European Union quickly criticized this "Anti-Secession Law," stating that the EU opposes any use of force and asks all parties to "avoid any unilateral action which might rekindle tensions."[22]

U.K. Foreign Secretary Jack Straw stated that this new PRC law has "created quite a difficult political environment."[23] The PRC move appeared to strengthen U.S. arguments that lifting the embargo could send the wrong signal to Beijing, and that a PLA possibly equipped with improved EU-provided defense technologies could pose a threat to Taiwan and U.S. forces in Asia. A high-level EU delegation to Washington in mid-March 2005 failed to convince U.S. officials and Members of Congress that existing EU plans for tighter export controls would sufficiently constrain arms sales to China. Lingering European human rights concerns about China also appear to be causing some EU members to consider postponing the decision on the arms embargo.[24]

As a result, some observers speculate that the EU's decision on its arms embargo on China may now be delayed until at least 2006. The United Kingdom will assume the EU's rotating six-month presidency in July 2005 and is unlikely to want the embargo lifted on its watch. (Luxembourg is the current holder of the EU presidency.) EU officials stress that if and when the embargo is lifted, its end would be accompanied by the simultaneous introduction of a package of measures, including an enhanced EU Code of Conduct on Arms Exports, to curtail more effectively European arms sales to China (and elsewhere), and to address U.S. concerns. Many analysts point out that the EU is politically committed to lifting the embargo, and believe that its end is ultimately only a matter of time. During a visit

---

[21] Translation of a portion of China's "Anti-Secession Law," adopted on March 14, 2005.

[22] Council of the European Union, "Declaration by the Presidency on Behalf of the European Union Concerning the Adoption of the "Anti-Secession Law" by the National People's Congress of the People's Republic of China," March 14, 2005.

[23] "EU Could Delay Lifting China Arms Ban," *Agence France Presse*, March 21, 2005. For background on the PRC's "Anti-Secession Law," see CRS Report RL32804, *China-U.S. Relations: Current Issues and Implications for U.S. Policy*, by Kerry Dumbaugh.

[24] Daniel Dombey, "EU Move on China Embargo Faces Delay," *Financial Times*, March 18, 2005; Judy Dempsey, "German Opposition Fights Against China," *International Herald Tribune*, March 21, 2005; Steven Weisman, "EU Said to Keep Embargo on Arms to China," *New York Times*, March 22, 2005.

to Brussels in mid-March 2005, PRC Foreign Minister Li Zhaoxing reportedly called again for an "early date" for lifting the "irrational" EU arms embargo against China.[25]

Administration's Position on the Embargo

The Bush Administration has opposed an end to the EU's arms embargo on China based on two major points. The first argument is that China's human rights violations that formed the basis for the embargo still exist. The second is that any expanded EU defense sales to China would damage U.S. security interests. The U.S. national interests threatened by a lifting of the arms embargo deal with security and value-projection — especially human rights and democracy. Whether the EU's arms embargo is significant or symbolic, lifting it would reduce the leverage of the United States and Europe on China to improve its human rights situation. From the viewpoint of U.S. concerns, a relaxation would send a signal to China that it can continue to violate international standards of human rights and that the United States, rather than China, is increasingly isolated in its views. The pressure would also lessen on the rulers in Beijing to reexamine the Tiananmen Crackdown. Since the late 1990s, the United States has urged China to "ratify and adhere to the International Covenant on Civil and Political Rights."[26] On the eve of the EU-China summit in December 2004, China acknowledged that it was still studying how to ratify the covenant.[27]

On January 28, 2004, a State Department spokesman acknowledged that the United States had held "senior-level" discussions with France and other EU countries about the issue of whether to lift the embargo on arms sales to China. He said, "certainly for the United States, our statutes and regulations prohibit sales of defense items to China. We believe that others should maintain their current arms embargoes as well. We believe that the U.S. and European prohibitions on arms sales are complementary, were imposed for the same reasons, specifically serious human rights abuses, and that those reasons remain valid today."[28] The Bush Administration reportedly also lodged diplomatic protests with EU members.[29]

At a hearing of the House International Relations Committee in February 2004, Representative Steve Chabot asked Secretary of State Colin Powell about the EU's reconsideration of the arms embargo against China, as supported by France. Powell responded that he raised this issue with the foreign ministers of France, Ireland, United Kingdom, and Germany, and expressed opposition to a change in the EU's policy at that time in light of the PLA's missiles arrayed against Taiwan, the

---

[25] "Arms Embargo Under Scrutiny as Foreign Minister Visits," *Europe Information*, March 19, 2005.

[26] Department of State, "State Department Hosts Bilateral Human Rights Dialogue with China," January 11, 1999.

[27] PRC Ministry of Foreign Affairs, press conference, December 7, 2004.

[28] Department of State, press briefing by Richard Boucher, January 28, 2004.

[29] Philip Pan, "U.S. Pressing EU to Uphold Arms Embargo Against China," *Washington Post*, January 31, 2004.

referendums on sensitive political issues then planned in Taiwan, and China's human rights conditions.[30]

A State Department spokesman argued on January 25, 2005, that the United States would continue to champion human rights in countries whether they are small or big, and that China's human rights situation not only has not improved, but has suffered "some negative developments."[31] On February 28, 2005, the State Department issued its report on human rights in 2004. It reported that China's human rights record "remained poor," and the Government continued to commit "numerous and serious abuses," although it amended the constitution to mention human rights for the first time. Moreover, "authorities were quick to suppress religious, political, and social groups that they perceived as threatening to government authority or national stability, especially before sensitive dates such as the 15th anniversary of the 1989 Tiananmen massacre and other significant political and religious occasions." The PRC government also used the international war on terrorism "as a pretext for cracking down harshly on suspected Uighur separatists expressing peaceful political dissent and on independent Muslim religious leaders."[32]

However, there is an apparent inconsistency in the Administration's claim that the EU is not taking into adequate consideration China's human rights conditions. On March 17, 2005, China released a Uighur woman named Rebiya Kadeer whom China arrested in 1999 in Xinjiang, and on the same day, the State Department announced that the Administration decided not to introduce a resolution on China's human rights abuses at the Human Rights Commission in Geneva, citing "some significant steps" on human rights. The State Department acknowledged that Kadeer's impending release was "a factor" in the decision. The decision raised a question about whether it undermined the U.S. position that the EU should not end the arms embargo because of human rights concerns. The State Department responded that the embargo was imposed because of the Tiananmen Crackdown, "and there are hundreds of demonstrators that remain imprisoned and there is a complete unwillingness to revisit or examine that incident in a critical light. So with regard to the conditions leading to the embargo, those have not changed at all, period."[33]

Regarding this U.S. argument, China's government remains unmoved in its position that it was justified in using military force in the Tiananmen Crackdown. The State Department's report on human rights noted that the PRC government "outlawed public commemoration of the 1989 Tiananmen massacre." Zhao Ziyang, the PRC premier at the time of the Tiananmen Crackdown who was put under house

---

[30] House International Relations Committee, "Hearing on the Budget Request for International Affairs," February 11, 2004.

[31] Department of State, press briefing, January 25, 2005.

[32] Department of State, "Country Reports on Human Rights Practices in 2004," February 28, 2005.

[33] Department of State, Daily Press Briefing, March 17, 2005; Jim Yardley, "China Frees Muslim Woman Days Ahead of Rice's Visit," *New York Times*, March 18, 2005; and "Freed China Prisoner Details 1999 Arrest," *AP/New York Times*, March 24, 2005.

arrest afterwards for not supporting the use of force, died on January 17, 2005. PRC rulers allowed his family to hold only a simple funeral on January 29, kept victims in house arrest, and deployed internal security forces to suppress voices of dissent calling for a reassessment of the brutal repression.[34] On March 22, 2005, hundreds of the former leaders of the 1989 pro-democracy movement, relatives of victims of the crackdown, and other activists wrote a letter to Secretary-General of the Council of the European Union and the President of the European Commission contending that "the human rights situation in China has not undergone any fundamental change since 1989." Moreover, they warned that "doing away with this sanction without corresponding improvements in human rights would send the wrong signal to the Chinese people, including especially those of us who lost loved ones, who are persecuted, and for all Chinese who continue to struggle for the ideal that inspired the 1989 movement."[35]

In early February 2005, newly-appointed Secretary of State Condoleezza Rice visited Brussels and expressed opposition to lifting the arms embargo on China and optimism that "the Europeans are listening to our concerns." She cited concerns about human rights and the military balance with China in Asia, namely, "the transfer of technology that might endanger in some way the very delicate military balance," while there are still American forces in the region.[36] Later that month, the Administration carried out diplomacy at the highest level with European allies. President Bush visited Brussels and cautioned that European defense-related transfers "would change the balance of relations between China and Taiwan."[37]

During Rice's first visit to Asia in March 2005 since becoming Secretary of State, she publicly warned that because the U.S. maintains a military presence in the Pacific region to support a stable environment for economic growth and democratic development, "anything that would appear to try and alter that balance would be of concern to us." She expressed concerns about the rise of China's military spending and potential military power with its "increasing sophistication." Rice stated that "the European Union should do nothing to contribute to a circumstance in which Chinese military modernization draws on European technology or even the political decision to suggest that it could draw on European technology when, in fact, it is the United States — not Europe — that has defended the Pacific."[38]

---

[34] Robert Marquand, "Zhao Remembered, But Cautiously," *Christian Science Monitor*, January 31, 2005; Joseph Kahn, "China Finds a Sort of Balance in Managing Memorial for Zhao," *New York Times*, January 31, 2005; Josephine Ma, "Dissidents Get Chance to Mourn China's Zhao Ziyang," *South China Morning Post*, February 8, 2005.

[35] "Open Letter to EU Secretary-General and President of the European Commission," March 22, 2005, distributed by the Project for the New American Century.

[36] Secretary of State Condoleezza Rice, "Remarks with European Commission President Jose Manuel Barroso and European Commissioner Benita Ferrero-Waldner After Their Meeting," Brussels, Belgium, February 9, 2005.

[37] White House, "President and Secretary General de Hoop Scheffer Discuss NATO Meeting," Belgium, February 22, 2005.

[38] Department of State, "Secretary of State's Remarks with South Korean Foreign Minister

(continued...)

Nonetheless, there are questions about the effectiveness of U.S. leverage and diplomacy, in part because of perceived mixed messages in the policy of engagement toward China, including the decision not to introduce a resolution at the Human Rights Commission. Also, while the United States has provided support to Taiwan's self-defense, it has adhered to the "one China" policy of working with the PRC on a range of international issues (with North Korean nuclear weapons frequently cited as a common problem). The United States also pursues Permanent Normal Trade Relations and significant trade with China, now ranked as the third largest U.S. trading partner (with bilateral trade valued at $231 billion in 2004 involving a deficit of $162 billion in China's favor).[39] There are questions about whether U.S. policy actually has promoted cross-strait stability, democracy, and human rights in China.[40] The tone in policy toward Taiwan changed from President Bush's declaration in April 2001 that the United States would do "whatever it took to help Taiwan defend herself" to his criticism in December 2003 (stated next to the visiting PRC premier) of Taiwan's leader for attempting to change the status quo. Some say the Administration has paid greater attention to arms sales to Taiwan than promotion of cross-strait dialogue.[41] U.S. criticism of European defense trade with China has been publicly harsher than that of Russian or Israeli sales to China. Successive Presidents have issued waivers of U.S. arms sanctions, as discussed above. Still, the Administration argues that U.S. engagement with China does not contribute dangerously to the PLA's buildup.

China's Accelerated Military Buildup

On the eve of the EU-China summit in December 2004, China's Foreign Ministry asserted that the EU's arms embargo should be ended, because it represented "political discrimination" against China. China argued that its demand on the EU to lift the arms embargo had nothing to do with buying "massive weapons from the EU," since China has "neither the capacity nor the intention to do so."[42]

Nonetheless, if the EU lifts its arms embargo on China, there are U.S. concerns that this step could:

- increase China's leverage if there are more competing bidders

---

[38] (...continued)
Ban Ki-Moon," Seoul, Korea, March 20, 2005.

[39] CRS Issue Brief IB91121, *China-U.S. Trade Issues*, by Wayne Morrison.

[40] For political issues in policy toward the PRC and Taiwan, see CRS Report RL32804, *China-U.S. Relations: Current Issues and Implications for U.S. Policy*; and CRS Issue Brief IB98034, *Taiwan: Recent Developments and U.S. Policy Choices*, by Kerry Dumbaugh.

[41] CRS Report RL30341, *China/Taiwan: Evolution of the "One China" Policy — Key Statements from Washington, Beijing, and Taipei* and CRS Report RL30957, *Taiwan: Major U.S. Arms Sales Since 1990*, by Shirley Kan. An example of one call for a proactive U.S. role in promoting cross-strait stability is: Kenneth Lieberthal, "Preventing a War Over Taiwan," *Foreign Affairs*, March/April 2005.

[42] PRC Ministry of Foreign Affairs, press conference, December 7, 2004.

- increase China's acquisitions of arms and military technology
- improve China's domestic defense industries
- strengthen China's ability to threaten or use force against Taiwan, U.S. allies, or U.S. forces
- increase China's weapons proliferation to unstable areas (in the Mideast, Asia, and Africa)
- increase China's rising influence regionally as well as globally.

One of China's major objectives has been faster military modernization, particularly in building up offensive capabilities for use against Taiwan and possible intervening U.S. forces and allies. In 1995 and 1996, the PLA conducted provocative military exercises and launches of short-range ballistic missiles into waters near Taiwan. To underscore serious U.S. concerns about China's willingness to use or threaten force, President Clinton deployed two aircraft carrier battle groups near Taiwan in March 1996. The United States is especially concerned that PLA modernization has accelerated after 1999. The Pentagon's report to Congress warned in May 2004 that "after close to 20 years of spectacular economic growth in China, Beijing's diplomatic successes, and steady improvement in the PLA's military capabilities, the cross-strait balance of power is steadily shifting in China's favor."[43] On February 16, 2005, the Director of Central Intelligence (DCI) Porter Goss testified that Beijing's military modernization and military buildup are tilting the balance of power in the Taiwan Strait and that improved PLA capabilities threaten U.S. forces in the region.[44] In particular, the PLA has engaged in a missile buildup, increasing its offensive short-range ballistic missiles at the rate of 50-75 per year, according to the Pentagon. Thus, the PLA has an estimated 600-675 such missiles targeted against Taiwan in 2005. The United States is also concerned that some of the PLA's missiles could hit U.S. forces based in Okinawa.

Rising Military Budgets

China's rising military budgets have contributed to the accelerated military modernization. Noting that the PRC's public military budget "markedly understates" actual defense-related expenditures (excluding categories such as weapons research and foreign arms purchases), the Pentagon's report to Congress on PRC military power estimated that China's total defense spending for 2003 was between $50 billion and $70 billion.[45] At that level, China had the third highest level of defense spending in the world (after the United States and Russia) and the highest level of defense spending in Asia (followed by Japan).

---

[43] Department of Defense, "Report on PRC Military Power," May 2004.

[44] Central Intelligence Agency, "Global Intelligence Challenges 2005: Meeting Long-term Challenges with a Long-term Strategy," testimony of DCI Porter Goss before the Senate Select Committee on Intelligence, statement prepared for delivery, February 16, 2005.

[45] The Defense Department estimates China's total military spending at 3.5 to 5 percent of gross domestic product (GDP). See Secretary of Defense, *Proliferation: Threat and Response*, 2001.

Even China's claimed defense budgets have indicated a priority in military upgrades. China's openly announced military budget projected for 2004 was about US$25 billion, a doubling of the official budget of about US$12.6 billion in 1999. On March 5, 2005, China announced a projected defense budget for 2005 of almost US$30 billion. (The chart shows the growth in billions of renminbi (RMB) of China's publicly announced — projected, not actual — military budgets from 1991 to 2005.) U.S. experts on the PLA do not consider China's publicly announced budget to be the full amount of resources given to the PLA. As one indicator of the priority placed on military modernization, China's publicly announced military budget has increased by double-digit percentages in nominal terms every year since 1989. In real terms (adjusted for inflation), China's military budget has increased every year since 1997 (after the Taiwan Strait crisis of 1995-1996), and increased by double-digit percentages in consecutive years since 1998.

Figure 1. China's Announced Military Budget

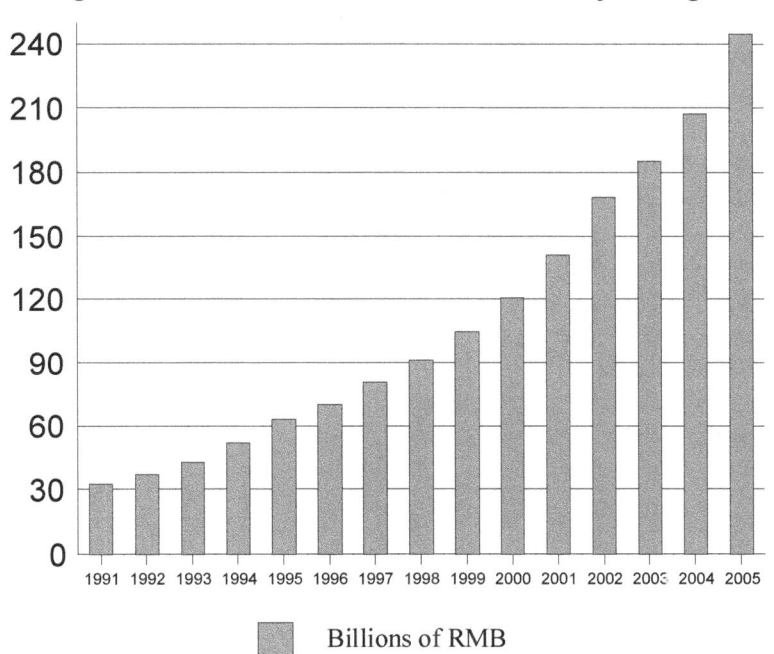

Billions of RMB

Military-Related Transfers to China

Greater resources allocated to defense also have allowed China to increase foreign arms purchases. After the United States, the EU, and other countries imposed arms sanctions on China in response to the crackdown on demonstrators in June 1989, Beijing turned to Moscow for advanced arms.[46] Since 1990, China has acquired significant advanced weaponry from the Soviet Union/Russia, its primary supplier, and has done so at an increased rate since 1999. The Pentagon's report on PRC military power informed Congress in 2004 that China purchased weapons from

---

[46] CRS Report RL30700, *China's Foreign Conventional Arms Acquisitions: Background and Analysis*, by Shirley Kan, Christopher Bolkcom, and Ronald O'Rourke.

Russia valued at about $1.2 billion a year during the 1990s, but such procurement increased to an annual average of twice that much since 1999. In 2004, sales to China accounted for 40-45 percent of Russia's total arms exports valued at $5.7 billion.[47] Thus, Russian arms sales to China were worth about $2.3-2.6 billion.

Since 1990, China's major arms purchases have included:

- 402 Russian Su-27 and Su-30 fighters (including 78 Su-27 fighters and trainers; 200 Su-27 fighters being co-produced in China; 76 Su-30MKK fighters; and 48 Su-30MK2 naval strike fighters for the PLA Navy)
- 12 Russian Kilo-class diesel-electric submarines
- 4 Russian Sovremenny-class destroyers
- Russian SA-10 and SA-15 air defense missile systems.

From a secondary supplier, Israel, China has ordered the Phalcon early warning radar (a sale Israel canceled in 2000 under U.S. opposition) and acquired Harpy anti-radiation attack drones. Moreover, Russian sources report that Beijing has pressured Moscow to shift from sales of weapons systems to transfers of new technology.[48]

With foreign arms sales and assistance, China has developed its domestic defense industries. New weapons programs in China include:

- Co-production of Su-27 (called J-11) fighters in China
- airborne warning and control system (AWACS) aircraft
- Luyang-class destroyers
- Type-054 frigates
- Song-class diesel-electric submarines
- Yuan-class diesel-electric submarines (unveiled in July 2004)
- Type-093 nuclear-powered attack submarines
- satellites and space launch vehicles.

The United States also is concerned about China's development of ballistic missiles, land-attack cruise missiles (LACMs), and anti-satellite (ASAT) weapons.

Meanwhile, European defense-related sales to China have increased. The EU reported that its total defense exports to China doubled from 210 million euros (about US$275 million) in 2002 to 416 million euros (about US$545 million) in 2003.[49] The value of such sales in 2003 was eight times that of sales in 2001 (worth 54 million euros).[50]

---

[47] "Russia: A Prosperous Year for Arms Exports," *Voyenno-Promyshlenny Kuryer* (Moscow), December 29, 2004, translated by FBIS.

[48] *Moscow Ekspert*, May 24, 2004, translated by FBIS.

[49] Daniel Dombey and James Blitz, "Doubts Over EU Policy on China Arms Sales," *Financial Times*, January 18, 2005.

[50] Tony Skinner and Michael Sirak, "EU Stands Firm on Lifting Embargo," *Jane's Defense*
(continued...)

Since the 1990s, European military-related sales to or cooperation with China have involved such items as: howitzers, helicopters, fire control radars, jet engines, avionics, diesel engines for naval ships and submarines, and satellites. For example, the U.K.'s Racal Electronics reportedly sold a Searchwater maritime reconnaissance radar for the PLA Navy's Y-8 airborne early warning aircraft, based on a 1996 contract for 6-8 radars. Rolls-Royce of the U.K. reportedly sold Spey engines for China's JH-7 naval strike fighters. Germany's MTU reportedly sold diesel engines for the PLA Navy's Luhai-class destroyer and Song-class submarines. Italy's Finmeccanica reportedly sold Grifo air combat radars for China's F-7 fighter that was also developed for Pakistan. France's S.E.M.T. Pielstick sold diesel engines for the PLA Navy's Type 054-class frigates, with a licence for co-production. Alcatel of France sold China the Chinasat-9 communications satellite, and Surrey Satellite Technology of the U.K. agreed to work on micro-satellites for China. (See **Tables 1 and 2** at the end of this report.)

Nicholas Burns, Under Secretary of State for Political Affairs, testified to Congress on April 14, 2005, that the Bush Administration has concerns about approvals for "current EU sales of military equipment to China," including fire control radars, aircraft engines, submarine technology, and maritime search radars. He characterized approvals for these items as "inconsistent" with the EU's Code of Conduct on military sales. Burns also expressed the American disagreement with European assurances that these transfers involved "non-lethal" items.[51]

Potential Benefits for China

In part because of European defense-related sales to China under the arms embargo thus far, there are concerns about potential gains for China if the embargo is lifted. China expressed its intention to gain military benefits from a removal of the EU's arms embargo. The PRC's own "Policy Paper on the EU" issued in October 2003 stated that the EU should lift its ban on arms sales to China at an early date so as to remove barriers to greater bilateral cooperation concerning defense industries and technology. The policy paper also called for high-level military exchanges; strategic consultation; exchanges of specialized military delegations; and exchanges in military training and education.[52]

The Defense Department's 2004 report to Congress on PRC military power warned against an end to the EU arms embargo. The report expressed concerns that lifting the embargo will provide China will "additional opportunities to acquire specific technologies from Western suppliers." According to the Pentagon, Russia

---

[50] (...continued)
Weekly, March 30, 2005.

[51] Joint Hearing of the House Committees on Armed Services and International Relations, "The National Security and Foreign Policy Implications for the United States of Arms Exports to the People's Republic of China by Member States of the European Union," April 14, 2005.

[52] *Xinhua* [New China News Agency], "China's EU Policy Paper," October 13, 2003.

would remain the PLA's primary supplier in the near-term, with Europe acting as "an emerging supplier."[53]

Some reports have speculated that China would attempt to purchase such weapon systems as airborne warning and control systems, jet engines, French Mirage fighters, and German submarines.[54] Others argue that China is unlikely to buy complete French fighters or German submarines, given that Russian platforms purchased since 1990 complement PLA weapons based on Soviet or Russian designs. European companies could sell more components and subsystems, particularly for command, control, and communications, and sensors, as they have under the embargo.[55] Former CIA Director James Woolsey judged that China does not need platforms from Europe but rather "command and control and reconnaissance to build systems of systems."[56] Such technologies could enhance the integration of weapons.

Without the political restraint of the arms embargo, a U.S. official has argued that the scale and sophistication of systems sold to China could significantly increase, and even non-lethal items, such as communication and command technologies, could raise the PLA's fighting power.[57] In any case, real or potential competition from European companies could provide China with stronger leverage to negotiate favorable deals for platforms and technology-transfers among Russian, Israeli, European, or other bidders for China's rising defense spending, especially absent strict European export controls. Russian President Vladimir Putin acknowledged this concern about the EU's lifting its arms embargo, saying "we sell a lot of arms to China. The less competitors on the Chinese market, the better." He also suggested future Russian-European cooperation in high-tech projects for China.[58]

A 2004 article in a Hong Kong journal with close ties to the PLA expressed some PRC aspirations for gaining access to "some of the world's best technological products" through Britain, Germany, and France. It said, "even though China is a major nuclear power, the many weaknesses of its conventional weaponry are precisely the ones that can be remedied through introducing new products from the EU." Nonetheless, the article judged that China is unlikely to engage in the great expense of replacing its domestic and Russian fighters and naval vessels with platforms up to Western standards nor make small deals that have little impact on warfighting capabilities. Rather, China is likely to seek technology-transfers and co-development and co-production. In particular, the article pointed to China's need for

---

[53] Department of Defense, "PRC Military Power," May 29, 2004.

[54] John Hill, "China Courts Friends in Europe," *Jane's Intelligence Review*, January 13, 2004; Craig Smith, "France Makes Headway in Push to Permit Arms Sales to China," *New York Times*, January 27, 2004.

[55] For example: Richard Bitzinger, "High Price to Pay for Overturning China Arms Ban," *Asia Times*, April 30, 2004.

[56] Quoted in *Aviation Week & Space Technology*, March 7, 2005.

[57] Susan Lawrence, "New Cracks in the Alliance," *Far Eastern Economic Review*, August 12, 2004.

[58] Russian Ministry of Foreign Affairs, "press conference following the four-country meeting among Russia, France, Germany, and Spain," March 21, 2005, translated by FBIS.

French missile technology, German submarine technology, British engine technology, advanced electronics and information technology, precision-guidance for missiles, sensors, lasers, radars, Galileo satellite navigational system, and stealth technology. Beyond foreign purchases, the article also stated that "China's main objective in importing advanced equipment is to enhance the research and development capabilities of its own national defense industry."[59]

The European Aeronautics Defense and Space Company (EADS) and Thales of France reportedly expressed interest in whether the arms embargo will be lifted, and Surrey Satellite Technology Ltd. of Britain argued that its satellite sales have no significant military utility, but speculated that the export licensing process could be faster without the embargo.[60] Companies in the aerospace industry (Airbus, Eurocopter, and Alcatel in particular) have forged increased business ties with China's aerospace defense industry.[61] Moreover, experts are watchful for the PLA Navy's acquisition of air-independent propulsion (AIP) technology for its new submarines and a radar system similar to the U.S. Aegis combat system on new destroyers.[62]

At the same time, European defense firms might decide against the potential costs to expanding defense business with China. For example, the head of the U.K.'s BAE Systems, Mike Turner, has stressed that his company would not jeopardize its lucrative business with the U.S. Defense Department because of possible sales in China.[63] While EADS might be interested in defense sales to China, Co-president Rainer Hertrich said that the company would not jeopardize its business in the United States by selling military equipment to China, conceding that "we have to take the United States into account in matters regarding China and Taiwan."[64] As China develops its defense or dual-use industries, there are additional concerns that it would copy Western technology and be a competitor in the long run. China has been a major arms supplier, particularly to the Mideast. In the aerospace sector, for example, even as China is seeking participation in Europe's Galileo satellite navigation project, an official of the China Aerospace Science and Technology Corporation said in November 2004 that China's intention is to establish its own global satellite navigation and positioning system.[65]

---

[59] Yu Yang, "What Weapons Will China Be Able to Purchase from Europe?" *Kuang Chiao Ching [Wide Angle]*, May 16, 2004, translated by FBIS.

[60] John Hill, "Europe Considers Ending Chinese Arms Embargo," *Jane's Intelligence Review*, June 1, 2004.

[61] Pierre Sparaco, "Chinese Encore," *Aviation Week & Space Technology*, June 21, 2004.

[62] Lyle Goldstein and William Murray, "China Emerges as a Maritime Power," *Jane's Intelligence Review*, October 1, 2004; *Ching Pao*, Hong Kong, December 1, 2003, translated by FBIS.

[63] Cited in *Aviation Week & Space Technology*, March 7, 2005.

[64] Cited in *Le Monde*, Paris, April 13, 2005, translated by FBIS.

[65] *Ta Kung Pao*, PRC-owned newspaper in Hong Kong, November 7, 2004, via FBIS.

EU's Perspectives

Both political and economic considerations are driving EU proclivities toward lifting the arms embargo on China. However, EU policymakers argue that the current EU arms embargo on China is largely symbolic and weak. Its end, they assert, will pave the way for a strengthened EU arms export control regime — including a revised and enhanced EU Code of Conduct on Arms Exports — that will be more effective in controlling arms sales not only to China, but also globally.

Political Motivations[66]

The EU is seeking to develop a "strategic partnership" with China. The EU views China as a rising political and economic power whose policies will have implications for global challenges ranging from weapons proliferation to environmental degradation. The EU believes that engagement with China on such issues would be mutually beneficial and hopes to further entrench China in the international system. This is as true for the U.K. and other EU member states that have been more hesitant about lifting the arms embargo on China as it is for France, Germany, and others that are more supportive. Some European leaders seem convinced that China shares their desires for a strong United Nations and a world governed by multilateral rules and institutions.

U.S. critics contend that a few EU members, such as France, are eager to engage more robustly with China in order to promote their vision of a multipolar world. Observers point out that China has made a concerted attempt to talk to the EU as an entity in recent years, and that this effort contrasts sharply with the perception of U.S. ambivalence toward further European integration and an enhanced EU role in international affairs. Most European officials reject the notion that the EU is seeking to counterbalance the United States. However, the EU views forging external relationships with other major powers, such as China, as a key part of building its Common Foreign and Security Policy (CFSP) and boosting the EU's role as an actor on the world stage.[67]

Many European policymakers perceive the arms embargo on China as a hindrance to developing closer EU-China ties. They concede that ending the embargo is the price demanded by China in order to deepen EU-China relations. But many agree with the Chinese position that the arms embargo lumps China in with other nations such as Burma and Zimbabwe, which are also subject to EU arms embargoes, and thus sends a negative signal about the state of EU-China relations. EU leaders argue that lifting the embargo on China would be a politically symbolic act, and that it would remove a psychological barrier to improved relations with

---

[66] For background on how the EU works and its governing institutions, see CRS Report RS21372, *The European Union: Questions and Answers*, by Kristin Archick.

[67] Reginald Dale, "Transatlantic Dispute Over Arming China," *International Herald Tribune*, July 15, 2005; Robin Niblett, "The United States, the European Union, and Lifting the Arms Embargo on China," CSIS Euro-Focus, September 30, 2004; Interviews of European and EU officials.

China. They stress repeatedly that their intention in lifting the embargo is not to sell more arms to China. In January 2005, Javier Solana, the EU's High Representative for CFSP, stated that lifting the arms embargo on China will be "more a political decision than a military one...it simply involves putting a stop to a political decision made at a specific time in the history of China, rather than a modification of military relations between the EU and China. It does not mean increasing arms exports."[68]

China's human rights record remains a concern for many EU member states, but others argue that China has evolved since 1989 and that the EU has engaged China in a meaningful human rights dialogue since 1996. They point out that the generation of leaders that ordered the Tiananmen crackdown is no longer in power, and they doubt that the EU arms embargo on China has made a difference on human rights conditions in China. The European Parliament opposes lifting the arms embargo on human rights grounds also, but the Parliament has no role in the decision, which rests solely with the member states.[69] The EU asserts that it will continue to pressure China to improve respect for human rights and the rule of law, despite an end to the embargo.

Commercial Interests

EU commercial interests are also at play. Some U.S. officials believe that France and Germany, among other member states, have been pushing to lift the arms ban chiefly to increase defense sales to China. As noted previously, total EU arms licensed for export to China have increased in recent years. Given that European defense companies are more dependent on arms exports than their U.S. counterparts, many analysts believe that some European leaders are eager to gain greater access to China's growing defense market. Some observers suggest that European frustration with what they view as limited opportunities in the U.S. defense market is fueling European interest in the Chinese defense market. French officials argue that European sales of weapons technologies to China could slow Beijing's efforts to develop its own capabilities.[70] On the other hand, some defense experts point out that EU companies and countries will have to weigh the benefits of selling arms to China against possible losses in the U.S. defense market, especially if Congress were to impose restrictions on U.S. procurement efforts from EU member states as a result.[71] (Also see the section on **Transatlantic Relations** below.)

---

[68] "Solana Suggests Early Warning System," Agence Europe, January 26, 2005.

[69] The EU's governing institutions do not correspond exactly to the traditional division of power in democratic governments. Rather, they embody the EU's dual supranational and intergovernmental character. The European Parliament has a decision-making role in several policy areas, but not in foreign or defense policy because member states retain sovereignty in these fields. The Parliament may issue non-binding opinions on foreign affairs issues. For more information, see CRS Report RS21998, *The European Parliament*, by Kristin Archick.

[70] Peter Spiegel and John Thornhill, "France Urges End To China Arms Embargo," *Financial Times*, February 15, 2005.

[71] William Matthews, "Who'll Get Hurt?," *Defense News*, March 14, 2005.

Some Europeans bristle at U.S. concerns regarding their potential arms sales to China. They point out that Washington is far less critical of Russian or Israeli arms exports to the PRC. They also note that Australia lifted its arms embargo on China in 1992, and Canada never imposed one following the Tiananmen Crackdown, but U.S. policymakers have not taken these countries to task.

Many observers assert that non-military economic objectives — such as deepening the EU's foreign investment profile and closing the EU's trade deficit with China — are also key motivating factors for several EU member states. They hope that lifting the embargo will encourage favorable procurement decisions by PRC authorities in areas such as commercial aircraft, automotives, civil engineering, and transportation infrastructure. For example, analysts point out that China's orders are crucial to the success of European-owned Airbus' A380 civilian jumbo jet, and PRC leaders have reportedly linked more orders for the A380 to an end to the arms ban. At the same time, some Europeans suspect that U.S. economic interests and concerns about growing European competition — especially in the commercial aircraft sector — might be motivating some U.S. opposition to an end to the EU's arms embargo on China.[72]

A Symbolic Embargo?

In any case, EU officials argue that the EU's current arms embargo on China is far from water-tight, and many view it as largely worthless. They point out that the language in the EU's 1989 political declaration calling for the embargo is extremely vague and each member state defines and implements it differently. Many countries, including the U.K. and France, have interpreted the embargo narrowly to cover lethal military items, but have continued to supply avionics, radar, and other military-related equipment. Nor does the embargo apply to dual-use items that can be used for both civil and military purposes.[73]

Nevertheless, some defense experts and U.S. officials claim that the embargo has exerted a restraining influence on many member states and thus, has prevented sales to China of weapons systems, such as fighters and submarines. European officials claim that they have no intention of selling their "next generation" weapons systems to China even if the embargo is lifted. French Defense Minister Michele Alliot-Marie has asserted that "we don't sell our state-of-the-art technologies to just anyone."[74] Some defense analysts, however, believe that an end to the EU embargo could cause a "ripple effect;" in this view, other countries already selling to China —

---

[72] Niblett, *Op. Cit.*; "Widening Business Opportunities Drive EU's Review of China Arms Embargo," *Aviation Week and Space Technology*, December 13, 2004; Mark Landler, "Europe Wants China Sales but Not Just of Weapons," *New York Times*, February 24, 2005; Discussions with European, EU, and U.S. officials.

[73] Judy Dempsey, "Britain Seeks To Tighten Rules on Arms To China," *International Herald Tribune*, March 9, 2005; Interviews of European, EU, and U.S. officials.

[74] Craig Smith, "In U.S. Visit, French Envoy Seeks Support on Arms Issues," *New York Times*, March 9, 2005.

such as Israel — may be compelled to sell even more advanced or high-tech items to China in order to remain competitive with European sellers.[75]

Code of Conduct and Arms Export Control Regime[76]

EU officials also stress that the arms embargo is neither the only nor the principal mechanism governing member states' military exports to China. Member states maintain their own national export controls, and in 1998, they agreed on the EU Code of Conduct on Arms Exports.[77] The Code sets out eight criteria for EU members to utilize when reviewing license requests and making decisions on whether or not to make an arms export. These can be summarized as follows:

(1) Consistency of export with international commitments arising from U.N., EU, or the Organization for Security and Cooperation in Europe (OSCE) arms embargoes;
(2) Risk that export would be used for internal repression or where the recipient country has engaged in serious violations of human rights;
(3) Risk that export would provoke or prolong armed conflicts;
(4) Risk of recipient using export to undermine regional peace and security;
(5) Effect of export on defense and national security interests of friends, allies, and other EU member states;
(6) Commitment of purchaser to fight terrorism and uphold international law;
(7) Risk of diversion to third parties or to a terrorist organization;
(8) Risk that export would undermine the sustainable development of the recipient country.

In June 2000, the EU adopted a Common List of Military Equipment covered by the EU Code in an effort to encourage standardization across the Union.[78] The EU asserts that the Code is intended to complement national arms export control legislation adopted by member states. Some EU members, such as Germany, have also reportedly translated the Code into their national legislation.

The Code also applies to dual-use goods if the end-user may be the recipient country's police or military forces. In addition, EU member states' exports of dual-use items are governed by an EU regulation that is directly applicable in EU member states; it establishes requirements that must be met and procedures to be followed for granting export licenses for dual-use goods. In June 2003, EU members also established common rules to control arms brokering to prevent circumvention of U.N., EU, or OSCE embargoes on arms exports and the criteria established in the EU Code. It calls on member states to put in place legal norms for lawful brokering

---

[75] Stephen Glain, "Bullets for Beijing," *Newsweek*, August 9, 2004.

[76] For more information, also see the Law Library of Congress Report No. 2005-01586, *European Union Arms Embargo on China*, by Theresa Papademetriou.

[77] The text of the EU's 1998 Code of Conduct is available on the EU's website [http://europa.eu.int/comm/external_relations/cfsp/sanctions/codeofconduct.pdf].

[78] The EU's Common List of Military Equipment was updated in November 2003. See [http://europa.eu.int/comm/external_relations/cfsp/sanctions/common-list.pdf].

activities, including obtaining written authorization prior to engaging in arms brokering and to keep records for a least 10 years.[79]

Many Europeans argue that the 1998 Code of Conduct has been much more instrumental in blocking arms sales to China, including high-tech and dual-use exports, than has the 1989 arms embargo, because the Code spells out specific criteria and sets up a denial notification and consultation mechanism, and other arms sales reporting requirements. These measures, they claim, exert considerable peer pressure on the member states to abide by the Code. For example, under the denial notification procedure, member states are required to transmit through diplomatic channels information on licenses refused and reasons for the denial. Before a member state authorizes a license for the same transaction that has already been refused by another member state, it must first consult the member state that rejected the license. If a member state decides to issue the license, it must inform the state that refused to grant authorization.

Nevertheless, numerous analysts have criticized the Code for containing several weaknesses and loopholes that militate against the Code being a strong regime in its current form. For example, some point out that although the Code sets up a denial notification procedure, there is no requirement for notification of licenses granted. Many also say that the Code's general reporting requirements do not provide sufficient transparency or accountability. The Code calls on each member state to prepare a confidential annual report, which is to be circulated by each member to the other EU states, on its defense exports and implementation of the Code. A consolidated public report is subsequently produced based on the submissions of individual EU members. However, the complete details of actual arms exports made by EU states are not set out in this public document, although it does provide values of arms export licenses issued and values of deliveries made, if available, by the exporting country. A supplier list is also provided, giving a total of sales denials made, but not what specific weapon sale was denied, nor to whom. Consequently, some analysts say that the Code's reporting requirements do not provide a full or clear picture of all EU arms exports; this, in turn, fuels suspicions that some EU member states may be understating the extent of defense deals already taking place with China.

Furthermore, critics argue that individual states have different arms trade licensing, data collecting and reporting practices, so there is often a lack of uniformity in reporting across the membership of the EU. For example, the EU's 2003 public report on the Code's implementation breaks down the export data by EU Common Military List category. For those states whose licensing systems categorize their arms export licenses in detail, it is possible to get a sense of what general types of military equipment are being licensed. However, the U.K. provides no detailed breakdown of its licenses because the way its standard export licenses are valued in its national licensing system currently preclude this. The same is true for Italy and

---

[79] The EU's regulation that governs exports of dual-use items is Council Regulation (EC) No 1334/2000 [http://europa.eu.int/comm/external_relations/cfsp/sanctions/1334.pdf]. The EU position on the control of arms brokering is Council Common Position 2003/468/CFSP [http://europa.eu.int/comm/external_relations/cfsp/sanctions/468.pdf].

the Czech Republic. France and Germany are able to break down the categories of their licenses for purposes of the EU report.[80]

Another complaint that some U.S. critics level against the Code is that it is neither legally binding nor enforceable. They are skeptical of EU arguments that the Code represents an effective politically binding commitment or that its reporting requirements dissuade member states from financially profitable arms exports. As evidence, they point to the increase in EU arms sales licenses to China over the last few years. EU officials maintain that although the Code is not legally binding, it is not voluntary either; all member states have agreed and are expected to implement the common foreign policy goals and moral imperative embodied in the Code.

Some analysts suggest that the Code should be transformed into an EU Common Position in the context of the EU's Common Foreign and Security Policy. The Treaty on European Union (the Maastricht Treaty) states that "member states shall ensure that their national policies conform to the common positions."[81] They believe this would lend added credibility to the Code and would effectively require its enforcement in national legislation. Others point out that enforcement would still be up to the competent authorities in the EU's member states, which could leave some differences in terms of implementation across the Union. More importantly, the decision to grant or deny any arms export would likely remain at the national discretion of each member, as the current Code states. For the foreseeable future, no member state would be willing to cede sovereignty over its national export control policies to the Union, or to agree to a sanctions scheme if one or more members were found non-compliant with the Code. In other situations in which EU members have agreed to enact penalties on their partners if they do not live up to their commitments — as with the financial requirements set out in the EU's Stability and Growth Pact for the EU's single currency — member states have been reluctant to actually impose such penalties for political reasons. However, the EU is working to revise and strengthen the Code to make it a more effective arms export control tool with better built-in peer pressure mechanisms (see below).[82]

EU's Plans and Other Options

As noted previously, the United States opposes an end to the EU's arms embargo on China and continues to urge the EU to maintain its embargo and strengthen export controls. In the event that the EU opts to overturn the embargo, EU

---

[80] The EU's annual reports on the Code of Conduct are published in the *Official Journal of the European Union*. Links to all of the annual reports may be found on the EU's website [http://ue.eu.int/cms3_fo/showPage.asp?id=408&lang=EN&mode=g]. For a critique of the annual reports, see Sibylle Bauer and Mark Bromley, *The European Union Code of Conduct on Arms Exports: Improving the Annual Report*, SIPRI Policy Paper No. 8 [http://editors.sipri.se/pubs/policypaper8.pdf], November 2004.

[81] See Article 15 of the Treaty on European Union. Available on the EU's website [http://europa.eu.int/eur-lex/lex/en/treaties/index.htm].

[82] Interviews with European, EU, and U.S. officials, January-March 2005.

officials insist that it will not lead to more arms sales to China. They point out that at the EU's December 2004 summit, the EU pledged that any eventual EU decision to end the arms embargo on China should not result in "an increase of arms exports from EU member states to China, neither in quantitative nor qualitative terms." This pledge has been dubbed the "standstill clause." In addition, the EU announced plans to adopt a revised Code of Conduct and a new "toolbox" — i.e., measures that will pertain to arms exports for countries, like China, that are emerging from an EU arms embargo. Both the revised Code and the "toolbox" seek to improve consultation, transparency, and accountability among member states. The United Kingdom and some smaller member states with human rights concerns about China have been key drivers behind these efforts aimed at strengthening the Code. They claim that the EU arms embargo on China will not be lifted until there is agreement on a more robust Code and on the "toolbox."[83]

The strengthened Code and the "toolbox" have reportedly been finalized at the technical level, but await political approval from EU leaders.[84] Publicly available details of the contents of both documents, however, are currently sketchy. Press reports and discussions with European officials suggest that provisions in the revised Code will seek to tighten requirements for technology transfers and the export of dual-use goods, and to clarify the Code's annual reporting requirements for member states. The "toolbox" is expected to call on member states to inform one another of defense export licenses granted as well as those denied to post-embargo countries (the current Code only requires notification of denials). To establish a baseline to judge whether some member states are violating the EU's "standstill clause" on China, the "toolbox" will also require EU member states to exchange information on all licenses approved and denied for the last five and three years respectively.

Many observers, however, doubt the credibility of the EU's "standstill clause" given what they view as strong European commercial interests in increasing arms sales to China. They question how compliance with the "standstill clause" or even a strengthened Code of Conduct will be measured or enforced. They also remain skeptical that EU member states possess the political will to significantly improve the Code or to increase information-sharing among themselves about their arms exports. Some member states have been resistant to sharing detailed information about licenses granted, arguing that company confidentiality must be respected. Furthermore, it is unclear how long the "toolbox" will apply. Some member states reportedly want its provisions requiring information-sharing on new licenses granted to be applicable for only a few years — perhaps three — while other members have advocated that the "toolbox" should remain in place for a decade at least.[85]

---

[83] Brussels European Council, Presidency Conclusions, December 17, 2004, *Op. Cit.*

[84] See European Union Fact Sheet, "China: Export Control Systems Fact Sheet," [http://www.eurunion.org/legislat/ChinExpContrSysts.doc].

[85] European Union Fact Sheet, "EU Arms and Dual Use Exports Policy and EU Embargo on China," February 2005 [http://europa.eu.int/comm/external_relations/us/bush/china.pdf]; Dempsey, *Op. Cit.*, Interviews of European, EU, and U.S. officials.

EU officials hope that their efforts to strengthen their arms export control regime will address U.S. concerns about lifting the arms embargo on China. Additional options the EU might consider to ameliorate U.S. concerns include:

- Seek explicit commitments from China on human rights. The EU claims it has been pressing China to ratify the U.N.'s 1976 International Covenant on Civil and Political Rights. The EU might also pursue the release of Chinese political prisoners. Press reports suggest that the EU may ask China for a "significant gesture" on human rights as a condition for lifting the embargo.[86]

- Seek commitments from China on nonproliferation of weapons of mass destruction and an agreement from China that it will refrain from re-exporting conventional arms and weapons systems obtained from EU member states.

- Establish a "no sell" list with the United States that would set out specific weapons and advanced technologies that neither side would export to China. This might be done in the context of establishing a regular U.S.-EU technical consultative mechanism to discuss military and dual-use technology exports to China. European officials are reportedly considering such a dialogue but maintain that it would have to be a two-way exchange of information.[87]

- Ensure that equipment would not be sold directly or indirectly to China's internal security forces, including the Ministry of Public Security and the paramilitary People's Armed Police (PAP), that could be used for repression of dissent and for crackdowns on Muslim populations (in the northwestern Xinjiang region) or Tibetans.

- Deepen involvement in the dispute across the Taiwan Strait to promote a peaceful resolution. In January 2004, German Foreign Minister Joschka Fischer acknowledged to reporters that Germany "sees a need for further discussion [with China] on human rights and on Taiwan."[88]

However, in his testimony to Congress on April 14, 2005, Under Secretary of State Nicholas Burns reported that the Administration will soon begin a Strategic Dialogue with the EU on the arms embargo on China and other Asian security issues, and he noted that the talks will not be a negotiation over terms for lifting the embargo.

---

[86] Katrin Bennhold and Graham Bowley, "EU May Tie China Arms Embargo to Human Rights," *International Herald Tribune*, April 13, 2005.

[87] "EU Finalizes Plan To Lift Arms Embargo on China," *Financial Times*, February 2, 2005; Discussions with European officials.

[88] "EU To Consider Lifting Arms Sales Ban on China," *Dow Jones Newswires/AP*, January 26, 2004.

Implications for U.S. Interests

Transatlantic Relations

Both U.S. and European officials believe that the EU's lifting of its arms embargo on China could torpedo recent U.S.-European efforts to revitalize the transatlantic relationship. If the EU ends the embargo and U.S. policymakers remain unconvinced that the EU's strengthened export control regime will sufficiently constrain European arms sales to China, some in Washington may take it as a sign that the EU cannot be trusted to be a responsible security partner. Given that 19 EU member states are also NATO allies, this could worsen U.S.-European tensions within the alliance. Amid transatlantic divisions over the war with Iraq and other foreign policy disputes, a number of U.S. officials and experts question the extent to which the European allies share U.S. interests and threat perceptions. A decision by 19 NATO allies to lift the EU's arms embargo on China in the absence of a stronger EU arms export control regime may further erode Washington's confidence in NATO's value or the allies' willingness to join with the United States in sharing the security burden not only within, but also outside of Europe. On the other hand, if the EU succeeds in creating a more robust arms export control regime with greater accountability and transparency that is more effective in curtailing arms sales to China than the current EU arms embargo, this may help to better protect U.S. interests in the region and demonstrate to U.S. skeptics that the European allies are committed to being credible and reliable security partners.

Lifting the embargo in order to pave the way for closer EU-China ties may also heighten U.S. concerns that the EU is seeking to create a multipolar world to constrain U.S. influence. EU members argue that they are not trying to strengthen China in order to balance or rival the United States. European policymakers admit that they did not adequately anticipate U.S. strategic concerns about ending the embargo, but that they are now trying to address U.S. worries. At the same time, some Europeans bristle at such vocal U.S. opposition because in their view, the Bush Administration has appeared uninterested until recently in consulting with or listening to its long-time allies on a range of international issues, from Iraq to climate change. They also worry that Washington's attempts to encourage one of more EU member states to veto ending the arms embargo on China may hinder EU efforts to develop a more common foreign policy.

Some U.S. and European officials and defense companies are concerned that if the EU moves ahead with ending the arms ban on China, this could impede U.S.-European defense cooperation on weapons systems and technology transfers. Over the years, the United States has developed defense arrangements with individual EU members states, either by the direct sales of U.S. defense articles, defense services, and military technology to them, or by engaging in joint cooperative ventures in the defense area. Overturning the EU embargo on China would probably increase U.S. fears that military equipment or sensitive weapons technologies sold to or shared with European countries might be re-exported to China.

Consequently, should the United States decide to impose severe restrictions on current or future sales or on defense cooperation, due to concerns raised by the lifting of the EU arms embargo on China, the effect on U.S.-EU defense industrial cooperation, and the quality and quantity of defense items sold to or purchased from EU countries could be significant. These potential effects are illustrated by the following:

- American sales of defense articles, services, and technology to individual states of the European Union have been notable. From 2000-2003, the United States concluded government-to-government arms sale agreements with Poland for $3.7 billion, with Greece for $3.3 billion, with the United Kingdom for $1.8 billion, and with Italy for $1.3 billion.[89] Regarding potential future sales as an example, the Defense Ministry of the United Kingdom has estimated that in coming years the value of new business in the U.K. for American defense contractors could approach $13 billion. This would be in addition to the defense supplies or programs for which American firms currently hold contracts.[90] U.S. defense industries have expressed concerns about the implications for their business prospects should the U.S. place significant restrictions on their exports to EU nations.[91]

- Between 2000 and 2004, the United States has imported from a single member of the EU, the United Kingdom, approximately $6 billion in defense products.[92]

- Various EU member states are suppliers of defense articles to the United States for incorporation into U.S. weapons systems. The supply of these defense articles could be curtailed or ended should given EU states choose to do so in a retaliatory response to U.S. restrictions on military sales to them. (See the text box below for examples of such weapons systems and the EU members that supply these defense articles to the United States). Although the United States could generally find domestic sources for defense components currently received from EU member states, this would require delays in production of given weapons systems and would increase costs until viable alternate U.S. domestic sources were identified and qualified, manufacturing facilities were created and placed under contract, and production to existing quality standards was initiated.

In addition, if the EU were to end its arms ban on China, most observers believe that neither the Bush Administration nor Congress would be likely to support exempting the U.K. or other EU member states from existing U.S. arms export controls. For several years efforts have been underway to exempt, in particular, the

---

[89] For more information, see CRS Report RL32689, *U.S. Arms Sales: Agreements with and Deliveries to Major Clients, 1996-2003*, by Richard F. Grimmett.

[90] Information provided by the Ministry of Defense of the United Kingdom.

[91] See for example, Matthews, *Op. Cit.*

[92] Information provided by the Ministry of Defense of the United Kingdom.

United Kingdom from the requirements of Section 38(j) of the U.S. Arms Export Control Act (AECA). This has generally been referred to as seeking a waiver from the International Traffic in Arms Regulations (ITAR).[93] Under such an exemption, unclassified defense items (equipment and intellectual materials) could be exported without the need for a U.S. export license. The rationale for such an exemption has been that certain allied countries with proven records of strict arms export controls, and common concerns about weapons proliferation, should be permitted to obtain U.S. defense articles and services with a minimum of regulatory review. Prior to the recent controversy over the EU embargo on China, the U.K. had not yet fully overcome Congressional concerns about the nature of U.K. export controls, including concerns about re-transfer controls. In October 2004, Congress passed a provision in the Ronald W. Reagan National Defense Authorization Act for FY2005 (P.L. 108-375) that directs expedited processing of U.K. requests for the purchase of U.S. defense articles or services, but does not provide for waiver of their review under U.S. law and regulations. (See the **Legislation** section below for details.)

Some speculate that European frustration with existing U.S. export controls on sensitive weapons technologies may play a role in the EU decision to lift or maintain the embargo. They suggest that some European defense policymakers are doubtful that they would ever obtain ITAR waivers. As a result, such European officials might feel that they have little to lose in this regard by agreeing to lift the EU arms embargo on China.[94]

---

[93] Section 38 of the Arms Export Control Act delegates authority to the President to promulgate regulations to govern the export and import of defense articles and defense services. Pursuant to this authority, the President has created the International Traffic in Arms Regulations (ITAR), which sets the rules and guidelines for U.S. arms exports, and contains the United States Munitions List, which in turn stipulates those items for which the U.S. Government must give approval prior to a U.S. company exporting any of them.

[94] "China and the EU," *The Economist*, May 15, 2004; Niblett, *Op. Cit.*, Discussions with U.S. and U.K. officials.

Key U.S. Weapons Systems with EU Suppliers

The **Patriot Advanced Capability (PAC-3) Missile** (the next generation upgrade to the Patriot Air Defense Systems used to destroy tactical ballistic missiles, cruise missiles or aircraft). The United Kingdom, Germany, the Netherlands and Belgium are EU member suppliers of component parts to the United States. The Department of Defense has stated that the capability to produce all PAC-3 components domestically does exist (though no assessment of production capacity has been announced) except for one — the lethality enhancer manufactured in Germany.

The **Tactical Tomahawk Missile** (the next generation surface and submarine-launched standoff weapon used by the Navy for critical, long-range precision strike missions). The United Kingdom and Italy are EU member suppliers of component parts. There are U.S. domestic suppliers with comparable capabilities available to produce the foreign source items, given some additional qualification time and cost. The Defense Department has not made public any assessment of the capacity of U.S. industry to manufacture these components in quantity.

The **Predator Unmanned Aerial Vehicle (UAV)** (a semi-autonomous, retaskable, unmanned aerial vehicle reconnaissance system providing surveillance, reconnaissance, target acquisition and direct strike capability to theater commanders). Belgium, Austria, and the United Kingdom are EU member suppliers of component parts. There are multiple U.S. domestic suppliers available to produce the foreign-supplied components, given additional qualification time and cost.

Source: Office of the Deputy Under Secretary of Defense for Industrial Policy, *Study on Impact of Foreign Sourcing of Systems*, January 2004.

Supporters of a strong transatlantic partnership caution that both the United States and its European allies must not allow the EU arms embargo issue to drive a wedge in the U.S.-European relationship. Some say this would fulfill what many China-watchers believe to be a PRC goal, i.e., to separate the United States from its traditional allies and increase U.S. isolation. Atlanticists argue that the United States and Europe stand a much better chance of addressing the challenges posed by China's rise if they work together rather than at cross purposes. Many suggest that despite the tensions surrounding the arms embargo issue, it has created an opportunity to establish a U.S.-European dialogue on security challenges in East Asia and their implications for U.S. and allied interests. On the other hand, they believe that if the United States sanctions European companies or restricts U.S.-European defense industrial cooperation in response to an end to the EU arms embargo on China, this would severely sour transatlantic relations. A significant transatlantic rift over the EU arms embargo on China could also hinder Washington's ability to gain allied support and cooperation on other global concerns ranging from countering terrorism to promoting peace in the Middle East to making the world trading system more open and efficient.

U.S. Policy Toward China

If the EU ended its arms embargo on China, particularly without a corresponding improvement in the U.S.-European dialogue, one implication might be a reduction in coordinated Western leverage on China to improve its human rights practices. Moreover, there might be less pressure on China's rulers to reexamine the Tiananmen Crackdown, a reexamination that would undermine China's justification for a possible military crackdown on pro-democracy demonstrators in the future. U.S. policy-makers might also review the priority placed on improving human rights conditions in China in the broader approach towards China.

On the security side, since the Nixon Administration in the early 1970s, the United States has promoted a policy of peaceful engagement with China, including vast economic ties, but remained vigilant to destabilizing moves by China. In the current Bush Administration, the U.S. National Security Strategy stated that "we welcome the emergence of a strong, peaceful, and prosperous China." At the same time, there are concerns. The same strategy also warned that "in pursuing advanced military capabilities that can threaten its neighbors in the Asia-Pacific region, China is following an outdated path that, in the end, will hamper its own pursuit of national greatness."[95]

Despite the engagement policy, there are concerns about China's rising economic, political, and military power, because of what some perceive as conflicting U.S.-China strategic interests for maintenance of global peace and stability. The Bush Administration's Quadrennial Defense Review (QDR) of 2001 declared that one U.S. security objective is to preclude hostile domination of critical areas, particularly Europe, Northeast Asia, the East Asian littoral, and the Middle East and Southwest Asia. Issued after the EP-3 aircraft collision crisis with China in April 2001,[96] the QDR cautioned that "although the United States will not face a peer competitor in the near future, the potential exists for regional powers to develop sufficient capabilities to threaten stability in regions critical to U.S. interests. In particular, Asia is gradually emerging as a region susceptible to large-scale military competition." While China is not named explicitly, the report points out that "the possibility exists that a military competitor with a formidable resource base will emerge in the region." Moreover, the report noted one particular area of concern: the "East Asia littoral" is defined as the region stretching from south of Japan through Australia and into the Bay of Bengal.[97]

Security implications would not be confined to the Asian region or the United States. The EU also has recognized that weapons nonproliferation is an issue with China. At the EU-China summit on December 8, 2004, they issued a "Joint Declaration on Nonproliferation and Arms Control." There is concern that foreign

---

[95] President George W. Bush, "The National Security Strategy of the United States of America," September 2002.

[96] See CRS Report RL30946, *China-U.S. Aircraft Collision Incident of April 2001: Assessments and Policy Implications*, coordinated by Shirley Kan.

[97] Department of Defense, "Quadrennial Defense Review Report," September 30, 2001.

cooperation with PRC defense-industrial corporations benefit and subsidize some that have engaged in weapons proliferation, including to unstable areas such as the Middle East. Moreover, as China obtains more advanced technology, it can sell its older equipment to poorer countries or those with problematic human rights records.

The United States has imposed sanctions on PRC entities, including some in the defense industries, with multiple sanctions imposed in certain cases on the same "serial proliferators." European companies have cooperated with some PRC organizations of concern for weapons proliferation. For example, Eurocopter signed an agreement with the Hafei Aviation Industry Company and China Aero-Technology Import-Export Corporation (CATIC) to assemble HC120 helicopters.[98] The State Department imposed sanctions for weapons proliferation on CATIC in May 2002 and December 2004. Italy's Iveco company has cooperated with North China Industries Corporation (NORINCO) to produce an anti-tank weapon. A defense-industrial organization, NORINCO has been a subject of U.S. sanctions on six occasions. U.S. sanctions also have been imposed on PRC entities in the shipbuilding and space launch industries. Alcatel's sale of the Chinasat-9 communication satellite undercuts U.S. sanctions for PRC weapons proliferation, which have prohibited the export of U.S. satellites to China.[99]

Furthermore, the EU's consideration of an end to its arms embargo on China has raised U.S. concerns about the EU's support for U.S. efforts to discourage an aggressive PRC posture in the Taiwan Strait and elsewhere in Asia. U.S. efforts to uphold Asian stability has fostered conditions benefitting U.S., European, Asian, and other economies. In particular, U.S. efforts have intensified since the summer of 2004 to focus on cross-strait dialogue as a priority, and U.S. officials consider 2005 to be a window of opportunity for resumption of cross-strait dialogue. Washington worries that, in ending the arms embargo, the EU could inadvertently send a different message from that of U.S. policy, which denies Beijing's claim to any justification to use force against Taiwan. According to this view, such a move would also undermine the EU's stated policy of supporting a peaceful resolution of the Taiwan question.

The attention on the EU's arms embargo could also lead to a review of whether U.S. arms sanctions on China should be maintained, eased, or tightened. A periodic issue concerns whether to issue further waivers of the sanctions imposed for the Tiananmen Crackdown, including for satellite exports (as discussed above in **U.S. Sanctions on Arms Sales to China**). In 2002, the State Department considered Boeing's request to export Chinook heavy-lift helicopters to China.[100] China's organizers and American exporters could urge transfers of U.S. equipment related to security surrounding the Olympics to be held in Beijing in 2008, equipment that also could be used for internal security.

---

[98] Pierre Sparaco, "Chinese Encore," *Aviation Week & Space Technology*, June 21, 2004.

[99] CRS Report RL31555, *China and Proliferation of Weapons of Mass Destruction and Missiles: Policy Issues*; and CRS Report 98-485, *China: Possible Missile Technology Transfers Under U.S. Satellite Export Policy — Actions and Chronology*, by Shirley Kan.

[100] Jason Sherman, "U.S. May Ease Utility Copter Export Rules," *Defense News*, April 8-14, 2002.

There is increasing concern in the U.S. government that China's military modernization is accelerated, offensive, and destabilizing, threatening U.S. forces and allies. Among U.S. allies, Japan, in particular, has increased concerns about the PLA's buildup. Japanese officials publicly have expressed opposition to the EU lifting its arms embargo, particularly after incidents that raised tensions. On November 10, 2004, a PLA Han-class submarine intruded into Japanese territorial waters, and Japan's Maritime Self-Defense Force deployed anti-submarine aircraft and destroyers to track the submarine. On January 22, 2005, Japan's Maritime Self-defense Forces tracked the PLA Navy's two Sovremenny-class destroyers in waters under Japanese surveillance.[101] Japanese Foreign Minister Nobutaka Machimura told the EU's top foreign policy official, Javier Solana, on February 8 that Japan opposes the lifting of the arms embargo, because that would have "a negative effect on security not only in Japan, but also in East Asia."[102] The United States and Japan issued a Joint Statement on February 19, 2005, which explicitly declared that they seek the common strategic objectives of encouraging China to "play a responsible and constructive role regionally as well as globally" and encouraging "the peaceful resolution of issues concerning the Taiwan Strait through dialogue."[103] Thus, the impact of U.S. diplomacy with the EU would affect U.S. security interests as well as those of allies, such as Japan (especially given the new level of U.S.-Japan allied coordination on security concerns).

Attention on the EU's arms embargo also raises questions about broader concerns over the range of arms suppliers to the PLA, including Russia, Europe, and Israel. (See **Tables 1 and 2** at the end of this report.) In response to the National Defense Authorization Act for FY2000, P.L. 106-65 (enacted on October 5, 1999), the Pentagon has submitted annual reports to Congress on PRC military power. In the National Defense Authorization Act for FY2002, P.L. 107-107 (enacted on December 28, 2001), Congress added a new requirement for the report to include a section on significant sales and transfers of military hardware, expertise, and technology to China. Congress did not limit the scope of this reporting requirement to transfers from Russia or other former Soviet states, as in the original language passed by the House. However, the new section of the report submitted in 2002, "Cooperation Between the Former Soviet Union and China," only discussed arms sales by former Soviet states, excluding Israel and other countries. The report submitted to Congress in 2003 did not have this section. The report in 2004 included a sub-section on "[Former Soviet Union] Arms Sales and Technology Transfers to China Since 1991," again excluding Israel. This report briefly raised concerns about an end to the EU's arms ban.

---

[101] *Yomiuri Shimbun*, Tokyo, January 25, 2005, via FBIS.

[102] *Tokyo Shimbun*, February 9, 2005, via FBIS.

[103] U.S. and Japanese Foreign and Defense Ministers issued the "Joint Statement of the U.S.-Japan Security Consultative Committee," February 19, 2005.

Options for U.S. Policy

Continue to Urge the EU to Maintain its Arms Embargo

Conveying specific U.S. concerns about China's ongoing human rights abuses to EU interlocutors may heighten concerns that lifting the embargo could increase internal repression in China. This argument may be especially cogent for member states such as Sweden, the Netherlands, and Ireland, which have strong human rights advocacy traditions. Some of the new EU members from Central and Eastern Europe may be more receptive to U.S. arguments that lifting the EU embargo could also damage U.S.-European relations in NATO. If the U.S. strategy, however, is perceived as trying to divide and weaken the EU, it could backfire and increase transatlantic tensions. Washington might also more systematically and publicly raise concerns about Russian and Israeli arms sales to China in order to deflect European complaints that EU members are being singled out for criticism.

Encourage the EU to Strengthen its Code of Conduct

The United States could encourage a significant strengthening of the European Union's Code of Conduct to enhance its transparency and provide EU member states with near-real-time notice of *prospective* arms sales to China *prior* to issuance of an export license. In this way, those EU members concerned about the negative implications of such a sale could bring peer pressure to bear within the EU arms control context sufficient to dissuade the prospective seller from agreeing to such a sale. Urging the EU to make the EU Code of Conduct, in its strengthened form, a Common Position, could also enhance its credibility as an instrument of arms exports control. The United States could also encourage the EU to incorporate into its own Military Control List the munitions lists of all major international arrangements, including the Wassenaar Arrangement Military Control lists. Fully encompassing all weapons lists in one place would further enhance the credibility of the EU's Code as the principal vehicle for EU arms exports control.

Promote a Cooperative U.S.-EU Strategy

The United States could promote a cooperative strategy toward China and possibly on East Asia more broadly. The United States could encourage the establishment of an institutionalized mechanism in which the United States, the EU, and possibly Japan, could engage in an on-going strategic dialogue on East Asia. EU and U.S. officials appear receptive to developing this sort of strategic dialogue. EU leaders view recent discussions with U.S. counterparts on China and the arms embargo as the first steps toward developing such a dialogue. Many Europeans say they were surprised by the strength of U.S. opposition to ending the EU ban because they did not view it as posing a threat to U.S. interests in the region. A sustained dialogue on East Asia may also enable Washington to draw its European allies and friends into deeper engagement on the question of Taiwan. Greater intelligence-sharing might be pursued.

Within this broad strategic dialogue, the United States could promote regular consultative meetings on potential U.S. and EU arms sales to the region. The United

States could in this way express to the EU what its greatest concerns may be regarding specific types of arms transfers to China. Such a vehicle would not intrude on the sovereignty of the EU member states by mandating a prohibited arms sales list for China, but would provide the EU, the United States, and possibly Japan, with a clear picture of what arms sales may be in prospect, and afford a private opportunity for the United States, in advance of any sale to China, to explain in detail its concerns about such a sale. In this way, it is possible that controversies over potentially problematic sales to China could be minimized or avoided.

Pursue Robust Bilateral Efforts on European Arms Exports

The United States could seek bilateral agreements with individual EU member states to constrain arms sales to China, and possibly to ban the transfer of sensitive U.S. weapons or technology to China. This might help ensure that U.S. interests are taken into consideration by each EU member state, given that national sovereignty concerns still limit the coordination of arms export control policies at the EU level. Such arrangements would also protect U.S. defense cooperation with those EU member states that have agreed with U.S. conditions. However, it is unclear whether EU member states would be receptive to such bilateral arrangements. Some may prefer an EU-wide agreement in order to bolster harmonization of export controls throughout the Union. Some member states might demand ITAR waivers or greater access to the U.S. defense market as the price of such bilateral agreements.

Engage with the European Parliament

Members of Congress could seek to play a role in shaping the transatlantic debate on East Asia by engaging in discussions with counterparts in the European Parliament through the existing Transatlantic Legislator's Dialogue. The European Parliament has passed several resolutions urging the EU to maintain the arms embargo. Although the Parliament does not have a formal role in the decision to maintain or lift the embargo, some analysts believe the Parliament has become an important forum for foreign policy debates in the EU. Members of Congress could encourage continued Parliamentarian vigilance of the status of the EU arms embargo on China, and of EU-China relations more broadly.

Retaliate to Protect U.S. National Security

Impose Restrictions on Sales of Defense Articles and Technology to EU Member States. If the EU lifts its arms embargo on China, many Members of Congress have asserted that they would be prepared to restrict U.S. sales of defense articles and technology to EU member states that sell certain defense items to China. This would help ensure that U.S. defense exports and advanced military technology are not re-directed to China. Such restrictions could be imposed by placing specific conditions, beyond those required by current U.S. law in the contracts for sale, by specifically stating that the contract would be null and void, should the buying company's nation make specific classes of arms sales or technology transfers to China. This could be done by a specific amendment to the Arms Export Control Act, by a free-standing bill, or through an amendment to an available legislative vehicle.

Impose Restrictions on U.S. Military Procurement from EU States.
The United States could place restrictions on defense industrial cooperation with EU states that make weapons sales to China the United States determines to be problematic. This could include suspension of cooperation with EU states currently participating in joint defense projects with the United States, such as the Joint Strike Fighter (JSF) program. It could also include termination of defense article purchases from EU states that are currently procured for integration into weapons systems produced by the United States, with the U.S. replacing the foreign defense article with one domestically produced.

Legislation

ITAR Waivers. On June 22, 2004, the Senate approved an amendment (S.Amdt. 3429) to the National Defense Authorization Act for FY2005 (S. 2400) that would have waived Section 38(j) of the Arms Export Control Act for the U.K. (and Australia). Section 38(j) requires that for a foreign country to become exempt from U.S. defense export licensing requirements it must have first concluded a "binding bilateral agreement" with the United States which obligates the foreign country to have or to establish a domestic defense export control regime consistent with the detailed guidelines set out in Sections 38(j) (1) and (2) of the Arms Export Control Act. In order to permit an export licensing exemption for the U.K., given the differences of its national export control system from that of the United States, Congress must waive Section 38(j). On October 9, 2004, the House and Senate approved a conference report on a bill that removed the Senate provision waiving Section 38(j), replacing it with a new provision (Section 1225 of H.R. 4200) which requires expedited processing of defense export licenses for the U.K. (and Australia), but does not exempt them from review. H.R. 4200 was signed into law (P.L. 108-375) on October 28, 2004.

Defense Procurement Sanctions. On May 25, 2005, the House passed H.R. 1815 the National Defense Authorization Act for FY2006 (H.R. 1815) with a provision (section 1212) that, among other things, forbids the Secretary of Defense from procuring "by contract or otherwise, any goods or services" from "any foreign person" the Secretary determines has "exported, transferred or otherwise provided to governmental or nongovernmental entities of the People's Republic of China any item or class of items on the United States Munitions List." Foreign persons determined by the Secretary of Defense to have engaged in any of the forbidden transactions with the PRC are not permitted to engage in procurement transactions with the Defense Department for five years. The Secretary can waive the sanctions of section 1212 of H.R. 1815 if he makes specific determinations in writing regarding the need to continue to procure specific goods or services from foreign persons who have engaged in forbidden transactions with the PRC.

In May 2004, the House passed its version of the Ronald W. Reagan National Defense Authorization Act for FY2005 (H.R. 4200), which included a provision to impose procurement sanctions against any foreign person that transfers certain military items to China. The Senate's bill did not have similar language, and the section was dropped in conference.

Resolutions Urging the EU to Keep the Embargo. On February 2, 2005, the House passed H.Res. 57 to urge the EU to maintain its arms embargo on China. On March 17, 2005, the Senate passed S.Res. 91, urging the EU to maintain its arms embargo on China.

Appendix: Non-Russian Military-Related Transfers to China

The following tables present information from unclassified reports on non-Russian military-related (including dual-use) transfers to China from European countries, Israel, and other secondary sources of supplies. **Table 1** reports on non-Russian systems that have been transferred or are under contracts. **Table 2** reports on non-Russian systems that have been reported as negotiated (not those in which China has shown interest), but contracts or transfers are not as evident as those in **Table 1**. The information should not be considered exhaustive, since commercial contracts for defense-related trade are closely guarded. CRS makes no claims as to whether such reported transfers violated any policies or contributed to the PLA's capabilities to threaten security interests of the United States or other countries.

Acronyms:
AAM   air-to-air missile
AEW   airborne early warning
SAM   surface-to-air missile
GPS   Global Positioning System
UAV   unmanned aerial vehicle

Table 1. China's Acquisitions under Reported Contracts for Military-Related Systems from Europe (Excluding Russia), Israel, and Others Since the 1990s

System/Technology (dual-use included)	Country (Company) as Reported Source of System or Technology	Citations and Comments
development of J-10 fighter (based on the Lavi)	Israel (Israel Aircraft Industries)	*Flight International*, Nov. 2-8, 1994: contract signed in 1992; *Los Angeles Times*, Dec. 28, 1994; Office of Naval Intelligence reported in 1996 that U.S. technology transferred through Israel; *People's Daily*, Apr. 9, 2003, PLAAF began testing.
Pack Howitzers	Italy (OTO-Breda Division of Alenia Difesa)	*Jane's Defense Weekly*, May 14, 1997: supplied two samples to the PLA, and the PRC apparently made copies instead of making further orders.

System/Technology (dual-use included)	Country (Company) as Reported Source of System or Technology	Citations and Comments
EC 120 helicopter	France/Germany/Spain (Eurocopter) & Singapore (Technologies Aerospace)	*People's Daily*, Nov. 21, 2003: agreement to assemble the helicopters in China, developed since 1993
Searchwater maritime reconnaissance radars for PLA Navy's Y-8 AEW aircraft	U.K. (Racal Thorn Defense of Racal Electronics)	*Defense News*, Aug. 5-11, 1996; contract for 6-8 radars; *Jane's Aircraft 2004-2005*: at least one Y-8 AEW aircraft.
PL-9 AAM/Python-3 AAM	Israel (Rafael)	*Aviation Week & Space Technology*, April 30, 2001: deployed on F-8 fighter that crashed into U.S. EP-3.
aircraft engines for K-8 jet trainer	Ukraine	DOD, PRC Military Power report, 2004.
components for missile systems	Belarus	DOD, PRC Military Power report, 2004.
Il-76 transport aircraft	Uzbekistan (Tashkent Aviation Production Association)	*Defense News*, Nov. 6, 2000: sold 10 in 1999; DOD, PRC Military Power report, 2004.
Spey engines for JH-7 naval strike fighters (export version called FBC-1 Flying Leopard)	U.K. (Rolls-Royce)	*Jane's Aircraft 2004-2005*: Contracts since 1970s with initial sale of an estimated 50 engines; *Defense News*, Feb. 1, 1999; *Far Eastern Economic Review*, Jan. 24, 2002: in 2001, supplied up to 90 additional jet engines, based on a 1999 deal.
avionics for F-7 fighter	U.K. (GEC-Marconi)	[http://www.sinodefence.com] May 1, 2004: featured in export versions
gas turbine and diesel engines for the Luhai-class destroyer	Ukraine (gas turbines) and Germany (MTU) (diesels)	*Jane's Defense Weekly*, May 1, 2002; *Jane's Fighting Ships 2004-2005*.

System/Technology (dual-use included)	Country (Company) as Reported Source of System or Technology	Citations and Comments
Kolchuga passive radars	Ukraine (Topaz)	Statement of Ambassador of Ukraine in Ottawa, Nov. 14, 2002; *CNN*, Nov. 26, 2002; Fisher, 2004.
Grifo air combat radar in FC-1 multi-role fighter developed in China for Pakistan and in F-7 fighter for PLA Air Force	Italy (Galileo Avionica of Finmeccanica)	Fisher, 2002; www.sinodefence.com, May 1, 2004; Sina Com, Dec. 1, 2004; Company information from Galileo Avionica.
EL/M-2032 fire-control radar for FC-1 fighter	Israel (Israel Aircraft Industries, Elta unit)	*Jane's Defense Weekly*, July 4, 2001
Arriel engines for Z-9 and Z-11 helicopters	France (Turbomeca)	*Jane's Aircraft 2001-2002*; Turbomeca, press release, March 15, 2004.
transmission system for Medium Helicopter (Z-10)	Italy/U.K. (AgustaWestland)	*South China Morning Post*, March 23, 1999; *Aviation Week & Space Technology*, Apr. 5, 1999; *Jane's Defense Weekly*, May 8, 2002
rotor system for Medium Helicopter (Z-10)	France/Germany/Spain (Eurocopter of EADS)	*Jane's Defense Weekly*, May 8, 2002; *Jane's Aircraft 2001-2002*.
engines for Z-8 and Z-10 helicopters	Canada (Pratt and Whitney Canada, subsidiary of United Technologies)	*Jane's Defense Weekly*, May 8, 2002
DFH-4 communication satellite	France (Alcatel)	Alcatel, press release on new contract, Sept. 27, 2002
Harpy anti-radiation UAV	Israel (Israel Aircraft Industries)	*Washington Times*, July 2, 2002; DOD, PRC Military Power report, 2003; in 2004, U.S. asked Israel not to return some upgraded attack drones.

System/Technology (dual-use included)	Country (Company) as Reported Source of System or Technology	Citations and Comments
Series 396 SE diesel engines for Song-class (Type 039) submarines	Germany (MTU, belonging to DaimlerChrysler)	*Hong Kong Commercial Daily*, May 16, 2004; *Jane's Fighting Ships 2004-2005*; Goldstein and Murray; *Kanwa Defense Review*, Oct. 15, 2004: total of 22 engines delivered by October 2004.
PA6 STC diesel engines for first two Type 054-class frigates, with licensed co-production	France (S.E.M.T. Pielstick)	*Jane's Fighting Ships 2004-2005*; S.E.M.T. Pielstick's company news.
An-70 transports	Ukraine (Antonov)	*Jane's Defense Weekly*, Oct. 1, 2003: August 2003 MOU for co-production.
Co-development and production of Y-8F600 medium transports (based on An-12 transports)	Ukraine (Antonov)	*Jane's Aircraft 2004-2005*; *Kiev Narodna Armiya*, Feb. 18, 2005: contracted in 2002 and first flight scheduled for summer 2005.
Galileo satellite navigation system (separate from U.S. GPS)	European Commission (European Space Agency)	*Xinhua*, October 10, 2004; China signed agreement with EU to join Galileo.
development of medium (7-ton) helicopter	France/Germany/Spain (Eurocopter of EADS)	*China Daily*, Oct. 11, 2004; *Dow Jones*, Oct. 13, 2004; signed agreement for co-development.
Chinasat-9 communications satellite	France (Alcatel)	*Space News*, June 14, 2004; $145 million contract signed on June 11, 2004, for delivery in late 2006 for PRC launch.

System/Technology (dual-use included)	Country (Company) as Reported Source of System or Technology	Citations and Comments
Earth observation, remote-sensing micro-satellites with extra high-resolution (50-meters)	U.K. (Surrey Satellite Technology Ltd., part of Surrey University)	*Far Eastern Economic Review*, Jan. 24, 2002; *Jane's Intelligence Review*, June 1, 2004; *China Daily*, Nov. 9, 2004; DOD, PRC Military Power report, 2004; *Financial Times*, Mar. 6, 2005; launch planned for May 2005.
Cross-country 4X4 chassis built in China for NORINCO's Red Arrow anti-tank guided weapon	Italy (Iveco)	*Jane's Defense Weekly*, Nov. 10, 2004; NORINCO is a defense-industrial corporation under U.S. sanctions for weapons proliferation.

Table 2. China's Reported Negotiations for Military-Related Systems from Non-Russian Sources Since the 1990s

System/Technology (dual-use included)	Country (Company) as Reported Source of System or Technology	Citations and Comments
Phalcon AEW radar (installed on Russian Il-76)	Israel (Israeli Aircraft Industries)	*Flight International*, July 17-23, 1996; March 19-25, 1997; Israel canceled in July 2000, after the U.S. objected.
Argus AEW radar	U.K. (GEC-Marconi Avionics)	*Defense News*, Mar. 18-24, 1996; Aug. 5-11, 1996.
Python-4 AAM	Israel (Rafael)	*Flight International*, Sep. 24-30, 1997; *Defense News*, Dec. 8-14, 1997; Fisher, 2004
Barak naval SAM system	Israel (MBT, ELTA, Rafael)	*SpaceDaily/AFP*, June 27, 2000; Fisher, 2004.
Lahat laser homing anti-tank missile	Israel (Israel Aircraft Industries, MBT unit)	*SpaceDaily/AFP*, June 27, 2000.
Ehud air combat training system	Israel (Israel Aircraft Industries)	*SpaceDaily/AFP*, June 27, 2000; Fisher, 2004.
licensed production of Spey jet engines starting in 2005-2006	U.K. (Rolls-Royce)	*Defense News*, July 2-8, 2001: unclear if U.K. approved technology exports.
Slava-class cruiser	Ukraine	*Kanwa Intelligence Review*, Jan. 6, 2003.
Tavor assault weapons	Israel (Israel Military Industries)	*Defense News*, Dec. 15, 2003.
telecommunications satellites	Israel (Israel Aircraft Industries)	*Space News*, Jan. 20, 2003: deal signed on Jan. 17, 2002, for 2-8 satellites, but remained unfunded.
Vera anti-aircraft radar systems	Czech (Omnipol)	*Aerospace Daily*, April 20, 2004; *Washington Times*, May 26, 2004; *Flight International*, June 1-7, 2004: U.S. objected in 2004.
An-124 and An-225 heavy transport planes	Ukraine (Antonov)	*Jane's Defense Weekly*, September 29, 2004

System/Technology (dual-use included)	Country (Company) as Reported Source of System or Technology	Citations and Comments
Zubr landing ship technology	Ukraine	*Kanwa Defense Review*, Oct. 15, 2004

Notes (to supplement the citations above):

These tables were compiled by Shirley Kan, Specialist in National Security Policy.

Department of Defense (DOD), "Report to Congress on PRC Military Power," July 2003 and May 2004.

Fisher, Richard, "Zhuhai Airshow, November 3-8, 2002," Center for Security Policy, 2002.

Fisher, Richard, "Known and Projected PRC Weapons Acquisitions," table in a report for the U.S.-China Economic and Security Review Commission, January 2004.

Goldstein, Lyle and William Murray, "China Emerges as a Maritime Power," *Jane's Intelligence Review*, October 1, 2004.

Office of Naval Intelligence (ONI), "Worldwide Challenges to Naval Strike Warfare," 1996.